Swedes

T0266325

IN MINNESOTA

Anne Gillespie Lewis

Foreword by Bill Holm

MINNESOTA HISTORICAL SOCIETY PRESS

Publication of this book was supported, in part, with funds provided by the June D. Holmquist Publication Endowment Fund of the Minnesota Historical Society.

www.mnhs.org/mhspress

The Minnesota Historical Society Press is a member of the Association of American University Presses.

Manufactured in Canada

10 9 8 7 6 5 4 3 2 1

International Standard Book Number: 0-87351-478-5

Library of Congress Cataloging-in-Publication Data

Lewis, Anne Gillespie.
　　Swedes in Minnesota / Anne Gillespie Lewis ; foreword by Bill Holm.
　　　　p.　cm. — (The people of Minnesota)
　　Includes bibliographical references and index.
　　ISBN 0-87351-478-5 (pbk. : alk. paper)
　　　　1. Swedish Americans—Minnesota—History. 2. Swedish Americans—Minnesota—Social conditions. 3. Minnesota—History. 4. Minnesota—Ethnic relations. I. Title. II. Series.

F615.S23L49 2004
977.6'004397—dc22
　　　　　　　　　　　　　　　　　　　　　　　　　　　　　2003025876

This book was designed and set in type by Wendy Holdman, Stanton Publication Services, St. Paul, Minnesota; it was printed by Friesens, Altona, Manitoba.

Contents

Foreword

by Bill Holm

Human beings have not been clever students at learning any lessons from their three or four thousand odd years of recorded history. We repeat our mistakes from generation to generation with tedious regularity. But we ought to have learned at least one simple truth: that there is no word, no idea that is not a double-edged sword. Take, for example, the adjective *ethnic.* In one direction, it cuts upward, to show us the faces, the lives, the histories of our neighbors and ourselves. It shows us that we are not alone on this planet—that we are all rooted with deep tendrils growing down to our ancestors and the stories of how they came to be not *there,* but *here.* These tendrils are visible in our noses and cheekbones, our middle-aged diseases and discomforts, our food, our religious habits, our celebrations, our manner of grieving, our very names. The fact that here in Minnesota, at any rate, we mostly live together in civil harmony— showing sometimes affectionate curiosity, sometimes puzzled irritation but seldom murderous violence—speaks well for our progress as a community of neighbors, even as members of a civilized human tribe.

But early in this new century in America we have seen the dark blade of the ethnic sword made visible, and it has cut us to the quick. From at least one angle, our national wounds from terrorist attacks are an example of ethnicity gone mad, tribal loyalty whipped to fanatical hysteria, until it turns human beings into monstrous machines of mass murder. Few tribes own a guiltless history in this regard.

The 20th century did not see much progress toward solving the problem of ethnicity. Think of Turk and Armenian, German and Jew, Hutu and Tutsi, Protestant and Catholic, Albanian and Serb, French and Algerian—think of our own lynchings. We all hoped for better from the 21st century but may not get any reprieve at all from the tidal waves of violence and hatred.

As global capitalism breaks down the borders between nation-states, fanatical ethnicity rises to life like a hydra. Cheerful advertisements assure us that we are all a family—wearing the same pants, drinking the same pop, singing and going on line together as we spend. When we invoke *family*, we don't seem to remember well the ancient Greek family tragedies. We need to make not a family but a civil community of neighbors, who may neither spend nor look alike but share a desire for truthful history—an alert curiosity about the stories and the lives of our neighbors and a respect both for difference—and for privacy. We must get the metaphors right; we are neither brothers nor sisters here in Minnesota, nor even cousins. We are neighbors, all us *ethnics,* and that fact imposes on us a stricter obligation than blood and, to the degree to which we live up to it, makes us civilized.

As both Minnesotans and Americans, none of us can escape the fact that we *ethnics,* in historic terms, have hardly settled here for the length of a sneeze. Most of us have barely had time to lose the language of our ancestors or to produce protein-stuffed children half a foot taller than ourselves. What does a mere century or a little better amount to in history? Even the oldest settlers—the almost ur-inhabitants, the Dakota and Ojibwa—emigrated here from elsewhere on the continent. The Jeffers Petroglyphs in southwest Minnesota are probably the oldest evidence we have of any human habitation. They are still and will most likely remain only shadowy tellers of any historic truth about us. Who made this language? History is silent. The only clear facts scholars agree on about these mysterious pictures carved in hard red Sioux quartzite is that they were the work of neither of the current native tribes and can be scientifically dated only between the melting of the last glacier and the arrival of the first European settlers in the territory. They seem very old to the eye. It is good for us, I think, that our history begins not with certainty, but with mystery, cause for wonder rather than warfare.

In 1978, before the first edition of this ethnic survey appeared, a researcher came to Minneota to interview local people for information about the Icelanders. Tiny though their numbers, the Icelanders were a real ethnic group with their own language, history, and habits of mind. They settled in the late 19th century in three small clumps around Minneota. At that time, I could still introduce this researcher to a few old ladies born in Iceland and to a dozen children of immigrants who grew up with English as a second language, thus with thick accents. The old still prayed the Lord's Prayer in Icelandic, to them the language of Jesus himself, and a handful of people could still read the ancient poems and sagas in the leather-covered editions brought as treasures from the old country. But two decades have wiped out that primary source. The first generation is gone, only a few alert and alive in the second, and the third speaks only English—real Americans in hardly a century. What driblets of Icelandic blood remain are mixed with a little of this, a little of that. The old thorny names, so difficult to pronounce, have been respelled, then corrected for sound.

Is this the end of ethnicity? The complete meltdown into history evaporated into global marketing anonymity? I say no. On a late October day, a letter arrives from a housewife in Nevis, Minnesota. She's never met me, but she's been to Iceland now and met unknown cousins she found on an Internet genealogy search. The didactic voice in my books reminds her of her father's voice: "He could've said that. Are we *all* literary?" We've never met, she confesses, but she gives me enough of her family tree to convince me that we might be cousins fifteen generations back. She is descended, she says with pride, from the Icelandic law speaker in 1063, Gunnar the Wise. She knows now that she is not alone in history. She has shadowing names, even dates, in her very cells. She says—with more smug pride—that her vinarterta (an Icelandic immigrant prune cake that is often the last surviving ghost of the old country) is better than any she ate in Iceland. She invites me to sample a piece if I ever get to Nevis. Who says there is no profit and joy in ethnicity? That killjoy has obviously never tasted vinarterta!

I think what is happening in this letter, both psychologically and culturally, happens simultaneously in the lives of hundreds of thousands of Minnesotans and countless millions of Americans. Only the details differ, pilaf, jiaozi, fry bread, collards, latkes, or menudo rather than vinarterta, but the process and the object remain the same. We came to this cold flat place so far from the sea in wave after wave of immigration—filling up the steadily fewer empty places in this vast midsection of a continent—but for all of us, whatever the reason for our arrival: poverty, political upheaval, ambition—we check most of our history, and thus our inner life, at the door of the new world. For a while, old habits and even the language carry on, but by the third generation, history is lost. Yet America's history, much less Minnesota's, is so tiny, so new, so uncertain, so much composed of broken connections—and now of vapid media marketing—that we feel a loneliness for a history that stretches back further into the life of the planet. We want more cousins so that, in the best sense, we can be better neighbors. We can acquire interior weight that will keep us rooted in our new homes. That is why we need to read these essays on the ethnic history of Minnesota. We need to meet those neighbors and listen to new stories.

We need also the concrete underpinning of facts that they provide to give real body to our tribal myths if those myths are not to drift off into nostalgic vapor. Svenskarnas Dag and Santa Lucia Day will not tell us much about the old Sweden that disgorged so many of its poor to Minnesota. At the height of the Vietnam War, an old schoolmate of mine steeled his courage to confess to his stern Swedish father that he was thinking both of conscientious objection and, if that didn't work, escape to Canada. He expected patriotic disdain, even contempt. Instead the upright old man wept and cried, "So soon again!" He had left Sweden early in the century to avoid the compulsory military draft but told that history to none of his children. The history of our arrival here does not lose its nobility by being filled with draft-dodging, tubercular lungs, head lice, poverty, failure. It gains humanity. We are all members of a very big club—and not an exclusive one.

I grew up in western Minnesota surrounded by accents: Icelandic, Norwegian, Swedish, Belgian, Dutch, German, Polish, French Canadian, Irish, even a Yankee or two, a French Jewish doctor, and a Japanese chicken sexer in Dr. Kerr's chicken hatchery. As a boy, I thought that a fair-sized family of nations. Some of those tribes have declined almost to extinction, and new immigrants have come to replace them: Mexican, Somali, Hmong, and Balkan. Relations are sometimes awkward as the old ethnicities bump their aging dispositions against the new, forgetting that their own grandparents spoke English strangely, dressed in odd clothes, and ate foods that astonished and sometimes repulsed their neighbors. History does not cease moving at the exact moment we begin to occupy it comfortably.

I've taught many Laotian students in my freshman English classes at Southwest State University in Marshall. I always assign papers on family history. For many children of the fourth generation, the real stories have evaporated, but for the Hmong, they are very much alive—escape followed by gunfire, swimming the Mekong, a childhood in Thai refugee camps. One student brought a piece of his mother's intricate embroidery to class and translated its symbolic storytelling language for his classmates. Those native-born children of farmers will now be haunted for life by the dark water of the Mekong. Ethnic history is alive and surprisingly well in Minnesota.

Meanwhile the passion for connection—thus a craving for a deeper history—has blossomed grandly in my generation and the new one in front of it. A Canadian professional genealogist at work at an immigrant genealogical center at Hofsos in north Iceland assures me, as fact, that genealogy has surpassed, in raw numbers, both stamp and coin collecting as a hobby. What will it next overtake? Baseball cards? Rock and roll 45 rpms? It's a sport with a future, and these essays on ethnic history are part of the evidence of its success.

I've even bought a little house in Hofsos, thirty miles south of the Arctic Circle where in the endless summer light I watch loads of immigrant descendants from Canada and the United States arrive clutching old brown-tone photos, yellowed letters in languages they don't read, the misspelled name of Grandpa's farm. They feed their information into computers and comb through heavy books, hoping to find the history lost when their ancestors simplified their names at Ellis Island or in Quebec. To be ethnic, somehow, is to be human. Neither can we escape it, nor should we want to. You cannot interest yourself in the lives of your neighbors if you don't take sufficient interest in your own.

Minnesotans often jokingly describe their ethnic backgrounds as "mongrel"—a little of this, a little of that, who knows what? But what a gift to be a mongrel! So many ethnicities and so little time in life to track them down! You will have to read many of these essays to find out who was up to what, when. We should also note that every one of us on this planet is a mongrel, thank God. The mongrel is the strongest and longest lived of dogs—and of humans, too. Only the dead are pure—and then, only in memory, never in fact. Mongrels do not kill each other to maintain the pure ideology of the tribe. They just go on mating, acquiring a richer ethnic history with every passing generation. So I commend this series to you. Let me introduce you to your neighbors. May you find pleasure and wisdom in their company.

Swedes

IN MINNESOTA

Camping is not just a recent phenomenon—here a group in heavily Swedish Isanti County enjoys a picnic in front of a tent at Spectacle Lake, about 1910.

"WHY DO WE ONLY EAT this weird food on Christmas Eve?" the teenager asked, gazing at a table bearing Swedish potato sausage, meatballs, rice pudding, lingonberries, herring, rye and cardamom breads, fruit soup, pepparkakor, and spritz.[1] The answer was simple. His family, like hundreds of thousands of other people in Minnesota, is now several generations removed from the old homeland of Sweden. Yet many of them still feel the need to preserve this link with their ancestors.

This ancestral fare, dutifully replicated down through the generations, continues to evoke deep feelings. To start a virtual food fight in a gathering of Minnesota Swedes, ask for recipes for the old standards such as meatballs, rice pudding, cardamom bread, and limpa (Swedish rye bread). Someone in the crowd will be sure to shout out "lutfisk" and there will be both cheers and groans in response. Lutfisk is dried fish reconstituted in a lye solution, rinsed copiously in water and sometimes whitened with bleach, and finally presented to the family or other eager and not-so-eager eaters during the Christmas season. The Norwegians claim lutefisk (note the difference in spelling) as their own, but Swedes eat it, too, sometimes when they do not even like it. Churches and other Swedish-flavored institutions, such as the American Swedish Institute in Minneapolis, hold lutfisk/lutefisk suppers starting as early as September and continuing until spring.

Although a few Minnesota Swedes still make treasured family recipes from scratch, most buy their lutfisk in supermarkets or drive to the Day Fish Company in Isanti County for it. Likewise, they buy potato sausage and meatball mix for their Christmas Eve smörgåsbord at the dwindling number of shops that carry them, including Ingebretsen's and Ready Meats, both in Minneapolis.

There are many enthusiastic Minnesota Swedes who

Swedish Meatballs

Fall starts the church supper season. Many of the Swedish American churches and organizations have supper traditions that go back many decades, such as the *kroppkakor* (pork-filled dumplings) supper at Spring Lake Lutheran Church in North Branch. However, Swedish meatballs are a much more common dish on the Christmas spread. Lots of families have their own treasured recipes for Swedish meatballs. Here are two of them:

Arlene Gronvall's Meatballs

Arlene Gronvall, who lives in Richfield, got this recipe in her 1939 cooking class at South High School in Minneapolis. The meatballs are served at family meals every Christmas.

1 pound ground beef	½ small onion, grated
1 egg, beaten	1 teaspoon salt
½ cup dried bread crumbs	¼ teaspoon celery salt
¼ cup water, plus more water for baking meatballs	¼ teaspoon allspice
	pepper to taste

In a medium bowl, mix all ingredients together. Roll into one-inch balls and set close together in an 8-by-8-inch pan. Brown for 40 minutes in a preheated 425 oven, turning after 20 minutes. Reduce heat to 325, pour water in the pan to come half way up the meatballs, cover, and bake an additional 45 minutes, turning again after about 20 minutes.

Lorraine McGrath's Meatballs

½ pound ground beef	1 small onion, grated
½ pound ground veal	white pepper to taste
½ pound ground pork	½ to ¾ cup bread crumbs
1 egg	¼ to ½ cup whipping cream
1½ teaspoon salt	butter for browning

In a large bowl, mix all ingredients except whipping cream and butter together. Add enough whipping cream to make meatballs that are soft but hold their shape. Melt butter in a heavy frying pan and brown meatballs. Transfer meatballs to a dutch oven or heavy sauce pan. Add a little water to the pan to keep meatballs from burning. Cover and let "steam" over a low heat for about an hour, adding more water if necessary.

The Gronvall family gathered at Jim and Linda Gronvall's house in Lakeville for Christmas 2001. The traditional menu included meatballs made according to the recipe from Jim's mother, Arlene.

have an intense interest in their history and culture as well as the food, but they are few compared to the majority of those whose roots are in Sweden. With most of Minnesota's Swedish Americans—even among some who say they are "one hundred percent Swedish"—the actual memories of Sweden are gone, the language has largely disappeared, and there is little communication with relatives in the technologically advanced land that is 21st-century Sweden. Only the food and some community celebrations tie the majority of them to a country many of them have never seen.

Whatever their level of interest in and knowledge about Sweden, those who declare themselves Swedish by ancestry, according to the 2000 census, make Minnesota the most Swedish state in the United States both in percentage and numbers.[2] In 2000, 9.9% of Minnesotans said their ancestry was Swedish, nearly double the percentage in second-place North Dakota (5.0%). The actual number of Minnesotans—486,507—who said their ancestry was Swedish was higher than in California, where 459,897 declared they were of Swedish ancestry.

The "most Swedish" statistics can go on and on. Seven of the ten counties in the U.S. with the highest percent of Swedes are in Minnesota, with Kittson County, in the northwest corner of the state, on top at nearly 34%. Gloria Swanson, a Hallock resident and Norwegian American whose husband Leonard was Swedish, answered the question of whether she had ever visited Sweden with a droll response: "Why would I need to go there? I always felt I was in Sweden here."[3]

Cambridge leads the nation in places of more than 5,000 residents in percentage of Swedish ancestry (27%). Even the Twin Cities, which have had great influxes of immigrants from non-European countries in recent years, are still marked with a Swedish stamp—7.9% for Minneapolis and 6.4% for St. Paul. Compare those numbers to Chicago, whose Swedish-speaking population by the end of

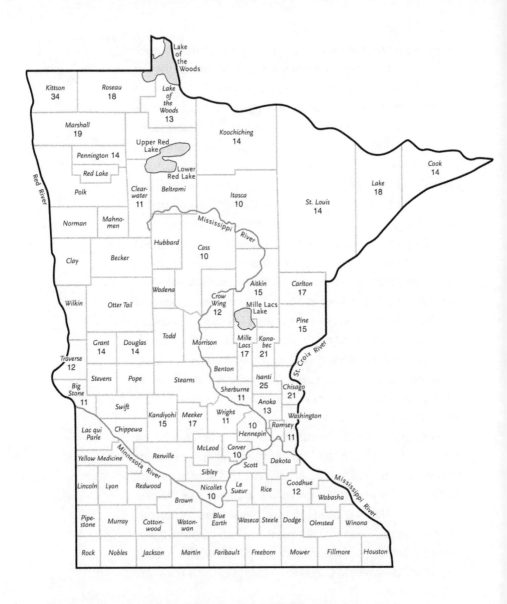

Minnesota counties where the greatest percentage of respondents reported Swedish ancestry (10% or more) according to the United States census for 2000

Swedish settlers probably shopped regularly at the Kittson County Farmers Cooperative Mercantile Company store (known as "the farmers' store"), pictured here in 1910, in Hallock, the county seat.

the 19th century was second only to Stockholm, Sweden; in the 2000 census, less than 1% of Chicagoans claimed Swedish ancestry. Even so, the number of those who declare themselves Swedes in Minnesota is shrinking. In the 1990 census, when the state's overall population was half a million less (4.4 million versus 4.9 million in 2000), the same question regarding ancestry was asked and 536,203 respondents said they were of Swedish ancestry.[4]

From 1845 when the mass movement of people from Sweden to North America began to 1930 when it ended, about 1,250,000 Swedes left their homes to settle in the New World. Only Ireland, Norway, and Iceland lost a greater percentage of their population during these years. By 1920, after which immigration slowed greatly, 23% of the state's foreign-born white residents were Swedes, with about half of them living in the Twin Cities.[5]

Early Immigration

Swedes have gravitated to Minnesota for more than 150 years. Jacob Falström, who found his way to what is now Minnesota about 1810, is generally regarded as the first Swede in the area. He married a Dakota woman, raised a family, and pursued a varied career as a fur trader and farmer in Washington County.

Although Minnesota Territory, organized in 1849, had a few Swedish residents before 1850, it was in that year that the first Swedes seeking land arrived in what is now Scan-

One of the earliest Swedish Lutheran churches in Minnesota was in Vasa in Goodhue County. The first pastor of the church was Eric Norelius. The church, pictured here in 1925, is part of the Vasa Historic District.

dia in Washington County. This settlement did not suc-
ceed, however, and the earliest lasting settlements were
begun several years later.

The first pioneers, despite being widely dispersed in
Minnesota, often knew or knew of each other. Eric Norelius, a Lutheran pastor who settled in Vasa in Goodhue
County, came to the United States with Joris Per Andersson, who is regarded as the founder of the Chisago Lakes
settlement. Norelius wrote about his decision to join the
Andersson group in his autobiography: "During the winter of 1850 an epidemic of 'America-Fever' began to spread
in Hassela parish and the surrounding region, as a result of
letters from friends and acquaintances who had gone to
America. Early in the spring it became known that a rather
wealthy farmer, Joris Per Anderson . . . in the western part
of Hassela parish, had decided to go to America. Soon other
people, old and young, married and unmarried, wanted to
go with him." Norelius and his brother, Anders, decided to
accompany Andersson. They left Hassela in Hälsingland
on July 18, 1850, finally arrived in New York on October 31,
and continued on to Illinois. The following year Andersson and some others journeyed from Illinois to start the
Chisago County settlement.[6] Unlike Andersson, most of
the early Chisago County immigrants were from Småland,
while the later arrivals,who settled in the northern part of
the county, came from other places in Sweden. The stream
of Swedes flowing into the region continued well into the
1880s.

Norelius maintained close ties with Andersson, but he
did not join him in Chisago County. Instead he went to
Vasa, Minnesota, where he became acquainted with another giant of Minnesota Swedish history, Hans Mattson.
A native of Skåne, Mattson fits the stereotype of the immigrant who made good. He arrived in St. Paul in September
1853 with a group of immigrants and was advised that good
land could be obtained near the new city of Red Wing in

Vasa

The village of Vasa, always small and by 2003 scarcely more than a church and its cemetery, produced a remarkable quartet of leaders—Hans Mattson, Eric Norelius, Swan J. Turnblad, and Alexander P. Anderson. Three were immigrants, and all spent at least part of their lives in Vasa. Mattson, a land agent for the railroad, a colonel in the Union army during the Civil War, Minnesota secretary of state (1870–72), and U.S. consul general to India (1881–83), put his stamp on the settlement. Norelius, a Lutheran pastor, was the first president of what became Gustavus Adolphus College, established many Lutheran churches, and helped organize the Augustana Synod. Both he and Mattson founded Swedish-language newspapers.

Norelius and his wife settled in their first house in Vasa, complete with homemade table and chairs. The young couple's lack of carpentry skills made for a comic moment when Mattson paid them a visit. Norelius recalled: "We made a table and some chairs by boring holes in some pieces of lumber and putting in some sticks to serve as legs. With a table cloth on the table and also some cloth covering on the chairs they looked very good. 'How splendid everything is,' said Hans Mattson . . . when he looked in one day. My wife invited him to have coffee with us, and as he sat drinking, the chair broke down with a crash and he fell backwards on the floor. No other harm was done and we could but laugh heartily at our poverty and elegance."

Hans Mattson, first Swedish American to hold state office as secretary of state, was later appointed consul to India. He is pictured in Indian dress in this photo taken about 1882 and used to make visiting cards.

Turnblad immigrated with his family to Vasa as a seven-year-old child in 1868. He moved to Minneapolis in 1879, went on to great success as the publisher of *Svenska Amerikanska Posten,* and built a 33-room mansion in south Minneapolis that became the home of the American Swedish Institute.

Anderson was born in Goodhue County to Swedish immigrant parents. He grew up on the family farm and taught in local schools before pursuing a university degree in science. His big discovery, which he patented, was the process for making puffed wheat and puffed rice. He later honored his roots by donating his family's Vasa farm to the Vasa Children's Home, an orphanage. Tower View Estate, Anderson's former home and laboratory on the outskirts of Red Wing, became the Anderson Center for Interdisciplinary Studies.

Alexander Anderson held a sample of puffed cereal in his laboratory in 1933.

Goodhue County. Guided by a man who knew the area, the party searched the deep valleys of the Cannon River for a suitable location. "[We] were not satisfied," Mattson wrote, "until we came upon the large prairie where Vasa is now situated. On this prairie we found the best soil and saw good oak woods in all directions." By the summer of 1854 at least ten Swedish families were living in the Vasa colony.[7]

Norelius arrived two years after the little settlement was founded. In his autobiography, which provides a glimpse of frontier life, he told of how he and his wife set to work making a home in Vasa: "As soon as the walls were up, we moved into our palace, without roof, floor, door, or window. The mattress was filled with hay and laid on a pile of shavings, and there we slept peacefully the first night, under the protecting hand of almighty God. When my wife shook out the mattress the next morning she found a snake in the hay; there were plenty of snakes in those days. The next day we made both ceiling and roof by stretching cloth over the house. On the plain board walls we put wall paper, and on the floor, which was a patchwork of odds and ends of lumber, we laid a cheap carpet that we had brought from Indiana. Thus we had a splendid house which had only one fault. It did not keep out the rain. Therefore we had to sleep under an umbrella on rainy nights."[8]

Another settlement was begun in 1854 near the Minnesota River four miles from the town of Carver. Originally called Oscar's Settlement, it became known as the

Pastor Eric Norelius and Inga Lotta Peterson Norelius in 1905

Union Colony and in 1858 was divided into the East and West Union Lutheran congregations. Many of the settlers, who were from the province of Västergötland, were drawn to the area by the so-called America letters, many of which praised the new homeland. These letters were important in creating similar concentrations of Swedes throughout the region. The son of one of the colony's founders wrote: "In our community . . . nearly all had come from the same district in Sweden. So completely had they transplanted a piece of Sweden to America that the names given to groves of trees and farmsteads were largely identical with those in the home district. This great emigration had been set in motion by a few personal letters."

Exploring Their Swedish Heritage

Are there typical "Minnesota Swedes?" You bet. Vernis and Corrine Olander and their little brother, Eddie, grew up on a farm in East Union in Carver County. "We're very Swedish," said Corrine. Their great-grandfather, John Adamson, who served in the Union army in the Civil War, was among many family members born in Sweden.

The Olander kids heard plenty of Swedish as children and were always aware of their heritage, but they were more excited about Saturday night trips to town, when each got a dime. "Vernis saved her money and bought a dress, but I always spent mine," said Corrine. The three loved it when their folks had to go to town and left them alone. "There were three things they told us we never should do," said Corrine, "Rock an empty rocking chair, because that meant a death in the family, open an umbrella in the house, because that meant bad luck, or climb up on the windmill. Well, as soon as they were down the drive, we rocked the chair, and the old umbrella was going up and down, and once Eddie climbed up on the windmill with the umbrella and opened it and waved it around."

Corrine, Eddie, and Vernis Olander, in 1929

Other settlements soon followed. Vista, named for the Småland parish from which most of its residents came, was settled in eastern Waseca County in 1857. Four groups of immigrants founded settlements north and south of Carver: Scandia (now Waconia); Götaholm on Swede Lake two miles south of Watertown; Scandia Grove (also known as the Lake Prairie Township) seven miles northwest of St. Peter; and New Sweden, later known as Bernadotte. Although Scandia Grove was on the edge of the prairie, early settlers emphasized the forest in their descriptions. One wrote: "There are about 1,200 acres of forest in our colony.... Four miles west of this forest are several thousand acres of prairie land at the congressional

Vernis and Corrine recall going to the East Union cemetery adjacent to the church with their mother to water the flowers on the graves. "We walked around and she would tell us about the different ones buried there. We still go to the cemetery to water the flowers. Most of the people buried there are our relatives, and now our husbands are there, too," said Vernis.

The three Olanders grew up, married, and had families. After Corrine and Vernis were widowed, they began doing research on their roots. They delved into the Adamson and Olander families, creating a massive genealogical record and scrapbook of newspaper articles, obituaries, and memorabilia for family members. Their children are also interested in their now-distant connection to Sweden. "When our grandmother came from Sweden, she didn't have any dishes, so the neighbors took up a collection and bought her a set of dishes. My son has them now, and he loves them. All our kids are aware of being Swedish," said Corrine.

When they retired, Corrine and Vernis took to the road and the air to track down their ancestors. They made two trips to Sweden to do research and meet relatives and were warmly welcomed and royally treated. They saw the tiny red house where their grandmother and her nine siblings were raised. And, of course, there were plenty of coffee parties. "They set such beautiful tables," said Corrine, "there wasn't a paper plate or a Styrofoam cup anywhere."

The ancestor they were especially fascinated by was John Adamson, who served four years in the Civil War without a major injury, although he was hospitalized in Little Rock, Arkansas, with sunstroke, ague, and diarrhea. "He came to the United States in 1859 and he enlisted in the army in 1861. I doubt that he could even speak English. How did he ever do it?" asked Corrine. Adamson, who served as a mule herder, was in Company A of the Fourth Minnesota Volunteer Infantry and also saw detached service with the 11th Ohio Battery. He was in the battles at Corinth and Vicksburg and was on Sherman's march through Georgia. Because he used the name John Hogstedt for a time before reverting to Adamson, he later had to fight to get his disability pension. "Being in the war was probably the biggest thing that ever happened to him, except for coming to America," said Corrine.

price ($1.25 per acre). This prairie has between one and two feet of black loam on a clay base, is free of stones, and is bordered on the south by large forests."[9]

Religious conflict was sometimes responsible for both emigration and the establishment of secondary settlements in Minnesota. Many nonconformist ideas had come to Sweden in the mid-19th century, and the state church tried to protect itself against such deviant doctrines by forbidding any private gathering for religious purposes. Offenders were punished by fines and prison sentences. Not surprisingly, many nonconformists were among the earliest emigrants from Sweden.

The intolerance of the Swedish church toward these groups sometimes survived the journey across the Atlantic. In 1856, for example, emigrants from Hälsingland started a Swedish Baptist congregation at Center City in Chisago County, which did not please the Swedish Lutheran majority. Before the year passed the Hälsingland congregation told the Minnesota Baptist Convention that it was "surrounded with a great number of our own nation who are all greatly opposed to our principles." Reluctant to stay in such a hostile environment, members moved to the Cambridge area in Isanti County. By 1860 the Center City Baptist Church was closed, and a new congregation, later known as the North Isanti Baptist Church, had been organized by 14 Hälsingland Baptists. In the late 1860s, large numbers of Lutherans settled in Isanti County. The first Swedish Lutheran church was built in Cambridge in 1866.[10]

More important than religious conflict in opening up new areas in this period was a provision in the Pre-emption Act of 1841 stipulating that an individual could stake a claim on government land before it was offered for sale. This meant that payment could be delayed until the government placed the land on the market. Many immigrants who arrived with little or no money saw this farm now–pay later opportunity as the best way to get started. Several small

Nellie Shulean, daughter of Swedish immigrants who settled first in Chisago and later in Isanti County was the first licensed physician in Isanti County. She practiced from the late 1880s until the 1920s and often made her rounds in a horse and buggy in the early days.

Swedish settlements established in 1856 and 1857 on the edge of the Minnesota prairies—including Litchfield and Swede Grove Townships in Meeker County and Kandiyohi and Eagle Lake in Kandiyohi County—are examples.

Some of the wilderness settlements beyond the settled edge of the frontier were short-lived because the Dakota Indians living on reservations along the Minnesota River began a war in August 1862 that caught the settlers completely off guard. Swedish settlers were among those killed in the Dakota Conflict. Those fortunate enough to escape fled eastward to safer areas behind the frontier. The fighting was quickly ended, but people were slow to return. Some never did; others, joined by later emigrants, decided to try again.[11]

Rural Settlements

The flood of Swedish immigrants did not start until the mid-1860s, when conditions in Sweden and Minnesota worked together to stimulate the great outpouring of Swedes. Almost 135,000 Swedes left their homes for the United States between 1863 and 1877, nearly 40% of them leaving in 1868 and 1869 after severe crop failures brought widespread hunger.

Families were still prominent in the emigration, but more young, single people joined the outflow. Large group migration was far less common, and economic motivations completely overshadowed religious ones. A majority of the emigrants were from rural areas, and they were still looking for land. Many were poor, however, and had little money with which to make a start.

Part of the lure was free land. Starting in 1862, millions of acres became available free to settlers under the Homestead Act, which guaranteed 160 acres to a settler or family who met certain conditions, including living on the land for five years. The railroads, which were rapidly reaching out from the Twin Cities, sold millions more acres at reasonable prices.

Many descendants of Swedish immigrants believe that their ancestors settled in Minnesota because it looked like Sweden, and many parts of the state do resemble it. Other parts—especially the prairie—certainly do not. Instead, the attraction of Minnesota initially may have been the transportation routes. From their arrival points of Montreal and New York City, immigrants could travel to Chicago by train and boat and then on to Minnesota, via the Mississippi River at first and later by rail. No other land on the frontier was so accessible from Chicago.

Railroads were the key to the location of new Swedish settlements, such as Sveadahl in Watonwan County (1868), Comfrey in Brown County, Dunnell in Martin County,

Cooperative Creameries

Swedish immigrants played an active part in making Minnesota a leading dairy state. Between 1860 and 1870, not only did the population of the state expand, but the number of cows in the state tripled. By 1899, Minnesota had 439 cooperative creameries. The number of co-ops increased into the 20th century. Nearly every small town had a co-op creamery.

Farmers in Shafer, Chisago County, nearly all of whom were Swedish immigrants, disagreed on the choice of manager for a creamery, and so for years the community had two separate creameries, one on the north end of town and the other on the south end. The two finally merged in 1919 after the north creamery burned.

In 1921, in order to improve marketing, quality, and price, about one-half (320 out of 622) of the existing creameries formed what became Land O' Lakes. Some of the old creamery buildings survive; the Isanti Cooperative Creamery, organized in 1914, reopened as the Creamery Café in 1979.

Wagons loaded with tubs of butter lined up in the street in front of the Farmers Cooperative Creamery in Milaca, about 1915. The creamery was one of hundreds in Minnesota that were run cooperatively by local farmers.

Louriston in Chippewa County (all in 1869), Balaton in Lyon County, and Worthington in Nobles County (both in 1871). In addition to offering easy access to unsettled prairie, the railroads provided employment for newly arrived immigrants.

The pastor of the Swedish Baptist Church recalled the birth of such a Swedish cluster at Worthington when he wrote: "In 1871, when the railroad was projected through the regions, several Swedish railroad workers who observed

The Swedish Mission Church in Worthington, later known as the Swedish Covenant Church, held a church-wide picnic in 1914. Art Grann, whose parents helped found the congregation, is second from left in the front row.

the fertility of the country and heard that there was land to be gotten took the opportunity to file for homesteads. . . . Others who had been made destitute by Indian raids farther North, came here to file on the land the same year."

Like most settlers, the Swedes had no experience with the prairie, but they accepted its challenges. A man who grew up near Sveadahl during the 1870s and 1880s remembered that "The snowstorms of the winter, which usually lasted three days in succession, were a deadly peril. Our first winter in Sveadahl was 'the terrible snowwinter,' when the snowdrifts reached as high as the roofs of the houses and stables."[12]

The main thrust of Swedish settlement, however, was along the principal line of the St. Paul and Pacific Railroad. Many Swedish and other Scandinavian settlements that sprang up along this line—including Cokato, Dassel, Litchfield, Swede Grove (now Grove City), Atwater, Lake Elizabeth, New London, and Mamre—owed their beginnings to Hans Mattson, a promoter of immigration for the state of Minnesota and a land agent for the railroad from 1866 to 1871. Swedes also settled in great numbers along the St. Paul and Pacific branch line, which ran northwest through St. Cloud and Alexandria to Moorhead.

As one of the founders of Vasa, Mattson not only influenced many Swedes from that colony to move to central Minnesota, he lured others directly from Sweden to the railroad lands in Meeker and Kandiyohi Counties. Later he worked for the Lake Superior and Mississippi Railroad and the Canadian government. Probably no other single individual had a greater influence on Swedish settlement patterns in Minnesota.[13]

Meanwhile, Swedish settlements in the St. Croix and Rum River Valleys continued to grow. While still more immigrants from Småland joined friends and relatives in the Chisago Lakes communities, the newer settlements, especially those in northern Chisago County, tended to be more mixed. In adjacent Isanti County, many immigrants came from upper Dalarna, starting in 1862 with Baptists from Orsa parish. The idea of emigrating spread from parish to parish, and by the famine year of 1868 nonconformists and Lutherans alike were streaming out of Dalarna.

The early Isanti connection led many to Minnesota. The first large group reached the Rum River Valley near Cambridge in 1866 from the parish of Rättvik in Dalarna, and many people from other parishes followed. A study of the Rättvik group, whose center was the Cambridge Lutheran

This horse, given to Cambridge by its sister city of Rättvik in Sweden some years ago, was restored by Wendell "Swede" Fridstrom at his body shop. It was later on display in front of the Cambridge Lutheran Church during the 2002 Swedish festival.

Church, found that certain organizational features of the Swedish parish were transplanted and consciously perpetuated, and Dalarna dialects were spoken there well into the 20th century.[14]

An important factor in stimulating Swedish settlement in the Red River Valley was the St. Paul, Minneapolis, and Manitoba Railroad (later the Great Northern), which reached Moorhead in 1871 and the Canadian border at St. Vincent in 1878. In 1879, a government land office was opened at Crookston. From the beginning, Swedish settlement was concentrated in the lower part of the valley, especially near Hallock in Kittson County. Early on, Swedes held positions of prominence there as both county and railroad officials. By 1890 at least half of the population of Kittson County was of Swedish descent; in Marshall County to the south probably at least a third of the people had Swedish forebears.[15]

Among the Marshall County immigrants was five-year-old Anna Lefrooth. There were stories and songs that made

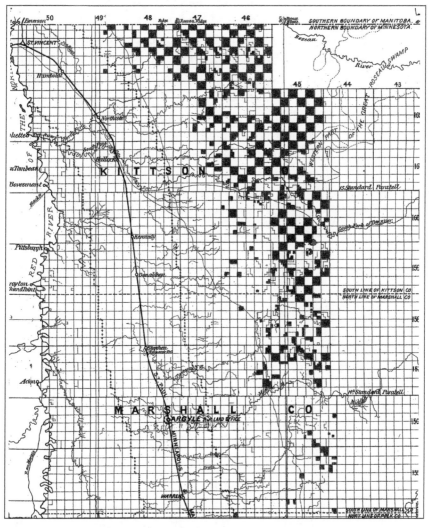

This map, green-and-white in the original, shows land offered for sale in eastern Marshall and Kittson Counties by the Great Northern Railway in 1895. Strandquist, where the Lefrooths settled, was named for Swedish immigrant John Erik Strandquist, but until 1905 it was also called Lund.

the Swedes think America's streets were paved with gold, but Anna expected it to be brightly colored. As she was getting ready to leave for America in 1883 from Västerbötten, Sweden, with her parents and siblings, she had seen a map of their destination in Minnesota. Apparently this was similar to the red- or green-and-white checked map put out later by the Great Northern that indicated which parcels of land were for sale and which were sold. "She told me when they were planning the trip at home that she saw the map, and she thought it was going to be so pretty because of the colors," recalled her grandson. Anna and her family took the train as close as they could get to their land. When they arrived in Stephen, Anna looked around and saw the bleak open land, not the pretty colored expanse that she had pictured. "She said she was so disappointed when they got off the train, and there was nothing there. They had to walk to their land, which was about ten miles away, and they went through a hayfield and spent the first night next to a haystack. They homesteaded west of Strandquist in Marshall County and lived in a sod house that first winter."[16]

Not all settlers were able to take the train to the Red River Valley settlements. Two 14-year-old boys—Charles J. Berg and Holger Mortenson—left behind to finish their confirmation classes in southern Minnesota, joined a wagon train of settlers and walked approximately 400 miles in 1880 to join their families in Kittson County, herding cattle along the way.[17]

From the bottomlands and terraces of the Red River valley, Swedish settlers moved eastward into the upper basin of the Roseau River, preceding the railroad, which did not reach Roseau and Warroad until 1908. With the forest settlements of the northeast, this district represented the last agricultural frontier of the Swedes in Minnesota.

Swedes were initially attracted to the forests by the lumber industry. As early as 1853 they bought land near the sawmill at Marine and worked as loggers in the St. Croix

John Ogren, an immigrant from Sweden, ran this logging camp on the Snake River near Mora, about 1905.

Valley. As their numbers increased, many followed the industry north. By 1890 Swedes and their descendants probably made up a quarter of Pine County's population. As lumbering moved from the St. Croix up the Snake River, it brought Swedes into Kanabec County. After the trees were cut, many immigrants from Jämtland and Ångermanland developed farms there, and even in the 1970s the county's population was predominantly of Swedish descent.

The early agricultural settlements in Isanti County meant that Swedes would figure prominently in lumbering along the upper Rum River. In Mille Lacs County extensive areas were also brought under the plow by Swedes in the 1890s, many of whom were sawmill workers from the Twin Cities. A large Swedish farming district subsequently developed around Milaca, Isle, and Opstead in Mille Lacs County and in Malmo Township in Aitkin County to the north. By 1930 Swedes made up 53% of Mille Lacs County's foreign born. Swedish settlements

Johannah Swanson won the footrace at this Fourth of July gathering of Swedish immigrants in northern Minnesota. Her husband, Adolph, was holding the tape and presumably cheering her on as she beat out the woman close behind her.

were small and scattered elsewhere in the pine forest. In the northeast, Swedish communities were often associated with those of Swede-Finns. The last Swedish rural settlement to be established in Minnesota began to develop about 1900 near Cook in northern St. Louis County.[18]

Young, single immigrants took advantage of the new job opportunities on Minnesota's iron ranges. Swedes were among the very first workers employed in the Soudan Mine and on the Duluth and Iron Range Railroad, which shipped the first Minnesota ore from the Vermilion Range

Swedish immigrant Carl Eric Wickman worked in the mines on the Iron Range before realizing that the miners needed transport. He and three partners formed the Hibbing Transportation Company, which after a period of growth and a series of mergers became the Greyhound Bus Company. Wickman is second from left in this photo from 1937.

Anders Gustaf Hammerstrom, in the middle of this group of men, worked in the Peter Grignon Shipyard and Marine Iron Company in Duluth when this photo was taken in about 1911. The company later became the Marine Iron and Ship Building Company. The tugboat *Excelsior,* which was repaired by the company, is in the background. Hammerstrom, a Swedish immigrant, later moved to Wisconsin and then to Minneapolis.

in 1884. Like most of the early miners, they were recruited from the Michigan ranges. Later, many Swedes worked on the giant Mesabi Range, where operations began in the early 1890s. Swedes rose quickly in the mining hierarchy; by 1900, with the Finns, they had largely replaced the Cornishmen as skilled workers and mine bosses. After the turn of the century the number of Swedish mine laborers declined as southern and eastern Europeans replaced them. Most remained in the area as mining company officials or learned new trades and became the carpenters, masons, plumbers, and plasterers of the iron range cities.

Swedes were particularly numerous in such important lumbering towns as Stillwater, which was close to the early rural Swedish settlements in the St. Croix valley, as well as in Brainerd and Cloquet. The Minnesota town with the highest percentage of Swedes in 1905 was Two Harbors, to which the Duluth, Missabe, and Iron Range Railroad carried ore for shipment east across the Great Lakes. Outside of the

Twin City metropolitan area, the largest number (6,920) of Swedes was in Duluth, the major iron- and grain-shipping port at the western end of Lake Superior, where a significant Swedish community had existed almost from the city's beginnings. As early as 1870, more than a decade before iron mining got under way, Swedes comprised a fifth of Duluth's population.

The towns of Alexandria, Moorhead, Red Wing, St. Peter, and Willmar flourished as service centers for many

A Ship Full of Swedes

In the burgeoning town of Duluth in 1869, the arrival of a ship was an exciting event. And so it was that a crowd gathered on June 16 to await the steamship Norman. *There were seldom eyewitness descriptions of the arrival of immigrants, but the writer for the new newspaper, the Duluth Weekly Minnesotian, was on hand to record a somewhat florid account of the ship and its passengers:*

The event of the week in Duluth was the arrival on Wednesday afternoon of the Steamer Norman of Leopold & Austrian's Chicago line, with nearly two hundred Swede immigrants and laborers for the Railroad....

As the Norman approached the dock ... the spectators upon the dock loudly cheered the boat, the officers and the go ahead owner, and cheered as well the sturdy and respectable looking immigrants just reaching their abiding place after their long travel of nearly 5,000 miles. Not only did the people on the dock cheer, but all along Minnesota Point, as the boat steamed within near view, the ladies waved their handkerchiefs and the men hurrahed while even at more distant points, at the head of Superior Bay near and around the hotel buildings, the hurrahs were caught up by the people until the doomed woods re-echoed with the shouts. Nor was the living mass on the steamship slow to respond ... their cheers on board responded to the cheers on shore.... Soon the immigrants poured on shore—and their myriad arks of baggage nearly covered the pier. A better looking set of Scandinavian immigrants, to be the first installment of what will finally be a mighty army, no one could have desired.... There were quite a number of families in the party—thirteen in all—with a goodly proportion of stout, healthy, and intelligent looking girls amongst them; and when it was announced that they were desirous of employment as house helps, you should have seen the celerity with which they were engaged and distributed around amongst the over worked matrons of Duluth.... The men, stout and hearty Scandinavians, were soon ranked in line on the upland opposite the dock and ... into working parties for the different jobs on the line of Mr. Branch's Railroad contract: moving off in marching order at once for the boarding shanties situated between here and Fond-du-lac: keeping step to the tune of a song of Faderland, that sound not unlike our John Brown tune in its notes.

There yet remained to be disposed of the *families* and their voluminous luggage. What to do with them was at first a serious and perplexing question. Though the President of the Railroad Company had directed the Construction Engineer more than two weeks ago to erect *immediately*

of the immigrant Swedes. Red Wing, in Goodhue County, was long a destination for immigrant Swedes, first because it was a steamboat stop on the Mississippi River and later because it was on the direct line from Chicago. Many greenhorns got off the train in Red Wing, bearing the names and addresses of Swedes who had gone before them, to seek temporary homes while looking for work. Willmar, Alexandria, and Moorhead were centers for the clusters of Swedish settlements that developed along rail

a "House for the accommodation of Emigrants" . . . nothing in the nature of such a "House" was ready—scarcely commenced.

The townspeople, including a few Swedes already in Duluth, took the families in, but the next edition of the Minnesotian *said that the house was sufficiently finished to shelter people. That structure was replaced by a building probably located on Michigan Street and 5th Ave. West in 1872.*

This house in Duluth for newly arrived immigrants, many of whom were Swedes, was conveniently located near both the railroad tracks and the docks.

lines. St. Peter served the Swedish agricultural settlements of Scandia Grove and Bernadotte and also became the home in 1876 of Gustavus Adolphus College, Minnesota's only Swedish Lutheran institution of higher education.[19]

Swedes in the Twin Cities

By the early 1890s young single adults dominated Swedish immigration, and many of them wound up in U.S. cities, not in rural areas. Minnesota, with its already large Swedish population, received a large share of these immigrants, who mostly settled in the Twin Cities. At the same time, young men and women from rural parts of the state were moving to the cities. Between 1880 and 1890 the number of Swedes in Minnesota swelled by some 60,000, giving it for the first time the largest Swedish-born population of any state. Of this increase, more than 26,000, or almost 45%, were in Minneapolis and St. Paul.

Young men took jobs in sawmills and flour mills, while many young women became domestic servants and workers for such firms as Munsingwear, which made underwear. Though many immigrants got their start in lowly jobs, they and their descendants realized the value of hard work and education, and many of them eventually became doctors, lawyers, bankers, contractors, business leaders, and other middle-class pillars of their communities.

The young, single Swedish emigrants around the turn of the century were attracted partly by the higher pay of the American labor market and partly by the encouragement of a large Swedish American community. By this time almost every young Swede had a relative somewhere in the United States whose tales of instant success were hard to resist. However, Sweden was becoming more industrialized, creating many job opportunities, and this surge of departures produced the first large-scale public opposition to emigration within Sweden.

The Carlson Sisters

The five Carlson sisters—Sophie, Hilda, Helen, Emma, and Augusta—all worked as servants for Governor Alexander Ramsey and his family in St. Paul in the late 1800s. Sophie was there the longest—from 1872 to 1885. The governor and his wife, Anna, often mentioned the Carlson girls in their letters, and Ramsey recorded driving Augusta to church in 1876 for a service in Swedish. The Ramseys also noted their absence, usually on visits to their father, Karl Grim, in Chisago County. The Carlsons apparently had an influence on the Ramsey grandchildren. The Ramseys' daughter, Marion Furness, wrote that her daughter, Laura, who was learning to talk, said, "Gulli[g], gulli[g],"—Swedish for "cute, cute." Sophie was a favorite of Anna Ramsey, and she inherited $1,000 in Mrs. Ramsey's will. When

The Carlson sisters—Helen, Augusta, Sophie, and Hilda (shown left to right) in 1909

Sophie left to get married, Ramsey wrote, "Sophy Carlson who has lived with us for more than 13 years & who was our Main dependance in the matter of house keeping greatly surprised us stating that she would marry and leave us."

A neighbor of their father, Chisago County farmer Carl Englund, wrote rather enviously about the industrious Carlson girls to his brother in Sweden in 1870. At that time, they apparently had other serving jobs in St. Paul. "(Karl) Grim lives at his brother's now. He came to visit me the day after Christmas. He bought 80 acres of land near his brother for $400. He has 4 girls who work in a city named Saint Paul. One earns $15 a month which helps so much. People who come here with so many children are wealthy—they'll never be as poor as when they come here if they are hard workers." The Carlsons sometimes made as much as $17 per month.

The connection between the Ramseys and the Carlsons did not end when the girls left one by one. Governor Ramsey talked of visiting Sophie, and she and some of the others returned on occasion to help out at the house.

The Swedish-born population of the state peaked in 1905 at just over 126,000. In Minnesota towns with a population of more than 3,000 persons, 7.6% of the population had been born in Sweden. Overall, Swedes were more urban than the population of the state as a whole; 44% of Swedish-born residents lived in cities, whereas only 32.7% of the state's total population did. And more than half of the urban-dwelling 44% lived in the Twin Cities. Almost 38,000 Swedes resided in Minneapolis and St. Paul, making

The Cuban Connection

Isanti County was only the first stop on S. P. Anderson's immigration journey. Anderson (the S. P. stood for "Stor Per" or "Big Pete") was part of a group of Swedish immigrants who moved from Isanti County and other places in the U.S. to Cuba to form a rather short-lived colony there in the early 20th century. Born in Sweden, S. P. grew potatoes in Minnesota but switched to raising sugar cane when he moved to Bayate, Cuba. Anderson and his wife spent several winters in Cuba before moving there permanently.

Colonists and friends gathered around an improvised table at Bayate, Cuba, about 1910. S. P. Anderson is seated, second from right.

The Cuban colony, officially named the Swedish Land and Colonization Company, was established by a Minneapolis physician, Dr. Alfred Lind, and several other investors in 1904. Lind, who was a Swedish immigrant himself, was one of the founders of Minneapolis' Swedish Hospital. He wrote that the majority of his medical practice involved restoring the health of fellow immigrants whose condition had deteriorated due to hard work and the harsh climate of Minnesota. About 125 Swedes or Swedish Americans lived in the Bayate community during the course of its existence. Plagued by financial difficulties, poor crops, and unsettled political conditions, the colony withered, and most of the colonists returned to Minnesota and elsewhere in the United States by 1917.

them the second largest urban concentration in the United States after Chicago with 63,000. Almost 7.5% of the Twin Cities population was Swedish born, a far larger percentage than in any other city of more than 100,000 people in the nation.[20] Emigration from Sweden placed a stamp on the Twin Cities, particularly Minneapolis, that survived into the 21st century.

Although Swedes in the Twin Cities tended to settle in clusters, they often intermingled with Norwegians and Danes. In 1910 Swedes constituted 61% of the Scandinavians born in the Twin Cities. Minneapolis came to be regarded as being more Swedish than St. Paul, but there was a time when Swedes were scarce enough for the pioneer Lutheran pastor Eric Norelius to write, "I set out on a trip west, through the 'great forest,' to the region now comprising Meeker and Kandiyohi counties. At that time [1861] there were no Swedes in Minneapolis, so there was no need to stop and preach there."

The first Swedish neighborhood in the Twin Cities was in the so-called *Svenska Dalen* or Swede Hollow on St. Paul's East Side. In the late 1850s Swedes began to move into the shantytown that had sprung up a decade earlier in the steep-sided valley carrying Phalen Creek to the Mississippi River. Milling and brewing industries, with their high demands for unskilled and semiskilled labor, were attracted to this valley in early days. The Swedes provided some of the needed labor. The squalid cluster of wooden huts spreading along the valley was a stepping stone to better things. For almost half a century Swede Hollow served as a funnel for newly arrived Swedish immigrants, and the name survived long after the Swedes were replaced by the Italians and Mexicans.

As success came to the early Swede Hollow residents, they spread north along Payne Avenue and up the bluff into Arlington Hills, where they were joined by later immigrants. At its height St. Paul's Swedish community stretched from the Mississippi River bluff north to Lake Phalen and the city's boundary with Maplewood. Payne Avenue, the neighborhood shopping street and the place for community celebrations, was its nerve center. One former merchant has

Swede Hollow, on St. Paul's East Side, was the first stop for many Swedish immigrants in the late 19th century. This view from 1898 shows the types of structures and the steep sides of the hollow. After several different immigrant groups passed through it, the shacks were cleared out and burned in December 1956.

been quoted as saying that if you did not speak Swedish you had no business on Payne Avenue.

The East Side community offered variety in job opportunities and residential areas. Although Hamm's Brewery was the largest single employer, retailing, crafts, a variety of small businesses, and the professions were also present. Property values rose as residents moved nearer the city limits, so it was possible to move up the social ladder without leaving the community. As people became more mobile, however, the distinctive Swedishness of the East Side declined. Car ownership enabled longer commutes and allowed friendship circles to expand beyond the neighborhood. While the East Side still had a sizable population of Swedish ancestry by the late 20th century, it was no longer the Swedish heart of the city.

Although the earliest Swedish settlement was in St. Paul, Minneapolis contained 70% of all the Swedes living in the Twin Cities by 1910. In 1930 Swedes were the largest foreign-born group in every section of Minneapolis except heavily Eastern European Wards 1 and 3 in the northeast part of the city.

Cedar Avenue, or Snoose Boulevard, catered to Scandinavian and other immigrants. In this view looking north about 1890, Dania Hall is the tall building on the right.

The substantial Swedish influx into Minneapolis began in the late 1860s with settlement near the corner of South Washington and 2nd Avenues. From there, the Scandinavian neighborhood spread eastward toward Cedar Avenue and Seven Corners. Immigrants who arrived fom 1880 to 1910 established Cedar-Riverside as the largest Scandinavian cluster in Minneapolis. A wide variety of lifestyles could be found there, from the down-and-outers who frequented the stretch of Cedar Avenue also known as Snoose Boulevard ("Snoose," is the phonetic version of the Swedish *snus,* meaning snuff) to the middle-class pillars of Augustana Lutheran Church at 7th Street South and 11th Avenue. Like St. Paul's East Side, Cedar-Riverside was a self-contained neighborhood, with residences, employ-

Hjalmar Peterson (center) better known as Olle I Skratthult, entertained Swedes here and on the road with his comic patter and songs. Members of his Hobo Orchestra were (standing, left to right) Bertil Danielson, Arthur Martinson, Werner Noreen, and Ted Johnson and Olga Lindgren-Peterson and Hazel Johnson (seated, left to right). His rendition of "Nikolina" sold 100,000 records.

ment, shopping, and entertainment within walking distance. Cedar Avenue was the main street, and it was lined with Scandinavian bars, hotels, rooming houses, banks, and bookstores. Dance halls abounded, and many a match was made on the dance floor. Cliff Brunzell, a violinist and band leader, remembered Cedar Avenue: "That's where the dance bands flourished. There were probably forty of them in Minneapolis and many of them were on or close to Cedar. Social life did center around the dance halls." In the late 1880s Dania Hall—sadly destroyed by fire in February 2000 as it was undergoing restoration—was built. The offerings of its upstairs theater and the nearby Southern Theater ranged from Strindberg to vaudeville and comedy. In the 1890s Pillsbury Settlement House was built in the area as a community center.

By the 1890s population pressure was pushing Scandinavians south of Franklin Avenue into the Powderhorn Park area and along the river into the Seward and Longfellow neighborhoods as far southeast as Minnehaha Park, the site of the annual Swedish midsummer festival, *Svenskarnas Dag*. When Cedar-Riverside began to decline in the 1920s during Prohibition, South Minneapolis became the heart of the city's Scandinavian community. Since the 1950s the expansion of the University of Minnesota to the river's west bank, the razing of part of the area to construct Interstate 35w, and the movement of students into houses on predominantly Scandinavian blocks dealt the final death blow to the old neighborhood.

Another large Scandinavian settlement grew up in Northeast Minneapolis, where a concentration of flour mills, breweries, foundries, railroad repair shops, and small industries led to the development of a distinctive blue-collar community. In the early 20th century, the boundary between the area's Scandinavian and Polish and Ukrainian people followed 5th Street, with the Scandinavians living to the east and the Slavs to the west. As late as 1930 Swedes were the largest single foreign-born group in Ward 9, the larger of the two Northeast wards. They dominated the Maple Hill-Columbia region, stretching from Broadway on the south to Columbia Park on the north, and the small Dogtown neighborhood south of Broadway. A stretch of Pierce Street was referred to as "Swede Alley." In 1980 in Northeast, Scandinavian neighborhoods were largely east of Fillmore and north of 18th Avenue. Early in the 21st century, the latest newcomers to Northeast included Hispanics and many multiethnic artists.

A third major Scandinavian community developed in Camden, in north Minneapolis, on the west side of the Mississippi River. A settlement grew up there around a shingle factory at the mouth of what came to be called Shingle Creek. Originally a Yankee enclave, it attracted Scandinavians and other immigrants who found jobs during the latter part of the 19th century in its lumberyards and brickworks. The C. A. Smith mill—owned by a Swedish immigrant despite his English-sounding name—employed many young immigrants, who often lived in one of Camden's boardinghouses.

By 1920 a heavily Scandinavian settlement extended from North 26th to 44th Avenues. From Lyndale Avenue to the river, the neighborhoods had a distinctly working-class flavor; to the west most residents owned their own homes and were comfortably well off. North of 44th Avenue, the landscape was still almost rural. Houses were small with big gardens, and the largely Scandinavian residents were young. In 1905 Camden (Ward 10) had a higher percentage of Swedish born than any other part of the city except the old Cedar-Riverside core. Two other small clusters were in the near north side of Minneapolis in the midst of mainly Jewish neighborhoods.[21]

The basic pattern of Scandinavian settlement both in the Twin Cities and in Minnesota had been established by 1913. Following a lull caused by World War I, Swedish emi-

The Nelson family, pictured here in 1905, ran a boardinghouse at 4301 Lyndale Ave. N. in the Camden neighborhood for many young single immigrants in the early 20th century.

gration rose briefly, but only about 100,000 people arrived during the 1920s. The 1930 census recorded only 90,623 Swedes, less than three-quarters of the peak population in Minnesota two decades earlier. After that, few people emigrated, and in some years those who left Sweden were outnumbered by those who returned. In the second half of the 20th century, emigration to the United States continued to be light. The few who did arrive in Minnesota did not

The Akerlund Photo Studio

For nearly half a century, from 1902 to 1950, August B. (Gust) Akerlund's camera recorded life in Cokato, Minnesota, a town whose residents were mainly Swedes like himself or Finns. Akerlund, born in 1872 in Hässjö parish in Västernorrland, Sweden, immigrated to the United States in 1893. After apprenticing to a photographer in Merrill, Wisconsin, Akerlund bought an existing photo studio in Cokato. Like other photographers, he was a chronicler of people's lives. He photographed babies, weddings, school and church groups, community festivals, and even the dead in their flower-bedecked caskets. Michael Worcester, director of the Akerlund Photo Studio and the Cokato Historical Museum, talked admiringly of Akerlund's skill. "I call him an artist," said Worcester. "He was very creative and he had an artistic eye."

Akerlund's thick Swedish accent sometimes baffled the children who sat for their portraits, and their parents often had to "interpret" his instructions. When Akerlund died in 1954, he left more than 14,000 negatives. Just as important as the treasure trove of negatives is the fact that Akerlund's studio survived and was restored to its 1905 appearance. The posing room of the studio is dominated by the large, north-facing skylight, which let in so much natural light that exposure times were much shorter than usual. In the restored studio, Akerlund's big camera faces the painted canvas backdrop, and a tattered dog puppet, used to coax smiles from reluctant children, sits atop the camera. Below it is a worn spot in the linoleum where Akerlund stood thousands of times to take the pictures. The studio is the only fully restored early 20th-century photo studio in Minnesota and is listed on the National Register of Historic Places.

Gust Akerlund's restored studio in 1996, showing the skylight, the painted backdrop, and the dog puppet perched on the camera

always identify with the long-established Swedish American community and did not appear to alter the imprint placed on the state by the great migration of the late 19th and early 20th centuries.[22]

From Swedish to American

Immigrant Swedes quickly adopted American clothes, but the adoption of the new language and integration into American life and existing institutions came at a slower pace. And, as with immigrants from any country, many Swedes had a longing for their distant homeland and family that lasted a lifetime.

The first Swedes to emigrate knew that they might never again see Sweden and the family left behind. Only a few early immigrants, such as *Svenska Amerikanska Posten* owner Swan J. Turnblad, could afford to return to Sweden on visits. For the majority, letters had to bridge the distance. A small number of them, such as Signe Olson Peterson, wrote poems to express their loneliness. Even those immigrants who arrived in the United States well into the 20th century sometimes did not go "home" for decades. In many cases, children and grandchildren of those who never made it back have journeyed to Sweden to become acquainted with the land of their heritage.[23]

In their early years in Minnesota, Swedish immigrants were drawn together and guaranteed familiarity through churches, fraternal and recreational groups, and music and other forms of entertainment aimed specifically at them. Gradually, the Swedes forged their own Swedish American, or more precisely Swedish Minnesotan, culture that borrowed from both the old and the new countries. The Swedes not only assimilated, their numbers—together with the other Scandinavian immigrants—were so large that in many ways they became one of the dominant cultures in the state.

Marlys Wickstrom at age 8 (back, center) with her parents, Emil and Agnes, and younger sister Karin

Marlys and Family

Children of immigrants sometimes felt the reverberations of that departure from the Old Country. Marlys Wickstrom, a resident of Isanti, remembered clearly how sad her father was when he received word that his mother had died in Sweden. "I was only three years old, and I remember feeling angry. I didn't even know I had another grandmother, and now she was dead. That feeling stayed with me, and 50 years later I wrote a poem about her for an English class I was taking at the community college." Here is a portion of it:

> In one instant she found and lost a grandmother.
> Her anger consumed her
> as she stomped down the hill
> on big, gray blocks of sidewalk.
> How could they have denied her this treasure?
> A grandmother, the best of all people,
> Why didn't they tell her?
> It is fifty years later, and the void remains . . .
> Does she know a granddaughter
> whom she never knew
> still mourns her loss?

The look of the newcomer was easy to change. Immigrants who arrived with a wardrobe that proclaimed that they were from the Old Country soon discarded it for American clothes. Hugo Nisbeth, a 19th-century Swedish traveler who visited Vasa for the traditional Swedish Midsummer Day, wrote later that he "looked in vain . . . for something of the Swedish folk dress, but not a trace of it was to be seen."[24]

Many Swedes retained their language for years after their emigration. Even in 2000, there were people in their 70s and older who said that their first language was Swedish and that they learned English in kindergarten or from older siblings. Still others, who spoke English from the start, told of parents and grandparents who used Swedish as a sort of secret code to talk about topics they did not want the children to understand. Many people mixed Swedish and English words together in sentences in a blend referred to as *mixat språk*.[25]

Most immigrants soon realized that they would have to learn English in order to deal with many merchants and most state and local government officials. Swedish immigrants did not question the need to know English and, unlike some German groups, they made no attempt to establish full-time Swedish primary schools, relying instead on summer schools, Sunday schools, and academies.[26]

In towns and cities English was a necessity. Lawrence Hammerstrom moved to a house on 29th and Harriet in Minneapolis from a farm near Maiden Rock, Wisconsin, when he was four years old in 1919. He did not have any playmates on the farm and thought he must have spoken Swedish with his parents and the other adults until the move. "After we

Lawrence Hammerstrom, shown on a horse shortly before he and his family left their farm in Wisconsin, spoke only Swedish until he moved to Minneapolis.

Salvation Army

The boom of the big bass drum on Cedar Avenue in Minneapolis' Seven Corners area summoned many Scandinavian immigrants to *Frälsningsarmén* (the Salvation Army) services in the late 19th and early 20th centuries. "In many cities it [the drum] became our church bells, calling the man on the street to our services," Edward O. Nelson wrote. And the beat was potent. According to one report, it was not unusual to see more than 3,000 people gathered for the services at Seven Corners.

For 52 years, the man carrying the bass drum along Cedar in Corps No. 4 was Otto Pearson, an immigrant from Sweden. His granddaughter, Mavis Teska, and her brother often tagged along to the outdoor services early Sunday evening.

The Scandinavian Department, separately administered from the rest of the Salvation Army, was a huge force among Swedish immigrants in Minnesota and elsewhere. There were once 94 corps—most of them Swedish-American—in the U.S. In 1888, Scandinavian corps opened on Cedar Avenue in Seven Corners and on Minnehaha Avenue on St. Paul's East Side. Eventually, there were more than a dozen corps in Minnesota, with five in Minneapolis.

There were several reasons for the Scandinavian Department's success, including providing the numerous single immigrants with a community as well as spiritual environment. "The Salvation Army was a 'home away from home' for these lonely and impoverished Swedish immigrants, and especially for the female domestic and the male sailor," according to William A. Johnson, who wrote a history of the Scandinavian Salvation Army. Many immigrant families and their descendants have served in the "Army" in Minnesota.

Women were an important part of the Salvation Army's work. An early "soldier," Annie Olson, was proud of her service: "I have had the privilege of opening two Swedish corps—Minneapolis 4 and St. Paul 2—where I saw many hard sinners seek salvation. I received the greatest blessing of all while I was stationed in Red Wing, Minnesota, where I was arrested three times and spent seven days and nights behind bars for preaching about Jesus Christ and his gospel on the streets."

Colonel Stig Franzén, born in Småland, Sweden, was the last leader of *Frälsningsarmén* in the central states. He took the Scandinavian banners down from the corps temples for the last time on January 1, 1965.

Many Swedish immigrants, such as Otto Pearson (back row, center), belonged to the Salvation Army in Sweden and in their new homeland of Minnesota.

moved in, the [English-speaking] boy next door came running over to meet me," said Hammerstrom. "He went back to his mother and said, 'I think that boy's crazy. I can't understand anything he said.'"27

The churches made the greatest effort to preserve Swedish as the spoken language of the home and local community. The principal religious bodies to which Swedish Americans belonged were the Augustana Lutheran Synod and the Mission Covenant, Swedish Baptist, and Swedish Methodist churches. In addition, the Salvation Army's Scandinavian Department was extremely active in Minnesota. All initially retained Swedish as the working language of the church. It is hard to overestimate the importance of the church as a community center, especially in rural areas of 19th-century Minnesota, where it forged the basic friendship circles in the society. By keeping Swedish not only as its liturgical language but as its social language as well, the church created an atmosphere in which Swedish was able to flourish, something individual families would have found very difficult to do.

Children of immigrants, who were receiving their education entirely in English-language public schools, received Sunday school instruction in Swedish. The Augustana Synod also established summer "week-day schools," sometimes known as "Swede schools." Patterned after the Swedish *folkskola*, they taught children to read the Bible and the catechism entirely in Swedish, using ABC books, Luther's Bible history, and songs.

The churches also opened secondary schools (then called academies), including Gustavus Adolphus at St. Peter, established by the Augustana synod; Bethel, in Roseville, started by the Swedish Baptist Church; and Minnehaha Academy in Minneapolis, which was begun by the Mission Covenant Church. Though originally designed to train ministers, they gradually expanded into more general education and also served to keep the Swedish language

David Stevenson, professor of planetary science at California Institute of Technology, lectured at the 1997 Nobel Conference at Gustavus Adolphus College. In 1963 the college signed an agreement with the Nobel Conference Board in Stockholm to sponsor an annual conference, which would focus on topics in science. The conference brings in world-class speakers, including 58 who have received the Nobel Prize.

Internationally known sculptor Paul Granlund worked on a piece in his studio at Gustavus Adolphus College, where he was sculptor in residence from 1871 to 1996. He received both Fulbright and Guggenheim scholarships and was chair of the sculpture department at the Minneapolis College of Art and Design. Gustavus has 30 of his works on campus.

and culture alive. At Gustavus Adolphus and Bethel, the academies were associated with colleges.

In 1883, the legislature passed a bill establishing a professorship in Scandinavian languages and literature at the University of Minnesota. In 1910, South High School in Minneapolis was the first secondary school in Minnesota to offer Swedish. By 1913, 10 high schools in the state offered Swedish, while there were only four in the rest of the

South High School students Lawrence Anderson, Ingrid Frisell, Elaine Dier, and Shirley Bartlett won an award for Swedish language study from Independent Order of Svithiod, a Swedish fraternal organization, in 1941.

country. Teaching Swedish was brought to an abrupt, but temporary, halt by antiforeign reaction during World War I. After the war, Swedish was taught at South High School in Minneapolis until 1973; at Minnehaha Academy classes in Swedish continued until 1988.[28]

Articles in the Swedish American press also helped to preserve Swedish. Many newspapers were organs of various churches, others represented political organizations, and some were purely literary in content. One survey revealed that at one time or another 106 Swedish-language papers were published in Minnesota. Most were short-lived, however, and many produced only one issue.

Three newspapers stand out as the most important in terms of their circulation and length of publication. *Veckobladet* (The Weekly Newspaper), published by the Mission Covenant church from 1884 to 1935, began as *Svenska Kristna Härolden* (The Swedish Christian Herald) and was also known for a time as *Minneapolis Weckoblad*. *Minnesota Stats Tidning* (Minnesota State Newspaper), founded by Hans Mattson in 1877, continued until 1939. It was always closely associated with the Augustana Synod. *Svenska Amerikanska Posten* (The Swedish American Post), begun in 1885

Swan Turnblad at his desk in the office of *Svenska Amerikanska Posten*

by the Swedish temperance movement, was the most widely read of the three. Under Swan J. Turnblad, who purchased it later, annual circulation exceeded 56,000 by 1915.

The golden era of Swedish-language publication in the United States was from 1910 to 1915. By 1918 only seven or eight Swedish-language papers were published in Minnesota, and just three survived into the 1930s. The last to go was *Svenska Amerikanska Posten,* which merged with the Chicago-based *Svenska Amerikanaren Tribunen* (The Swedish American Tribune). In its final issue of September 11, 1940, *Posten* pointed out that Minnesota was losing its only Swedish-language newspaper, stating that its purposes, as established and defined by Swan Turnblad, had been to promote "God's work, Prohibition, the advancement of the 'people,'" as well as "to foster Swedish culture in America and to spread the news."[29]

In spite of the efforts of the churches and the press, the use of Swedish in Minnesota declined, partly due to the halt of immigration when World War I began. Increasingly, Swedish Americans who had been educated in English regarded that as their mother tongue. Without the reinforcement of new immigrants, the older generations had a hard time convincing the younger ones of the importance of preserving the language and a distinctive Swedish culture. The hostile attitude of many Americans toward anything foreign during World War I, which severely weakened the Swedish language's position in the home and church, made their task still harder.

The decline of the Swedish-language press between World Wars I and II was paralleled by a more gradual discontinuation of the use of Swedish in the churches. As early as 1880 the exclusive use of Swedish within the Augustana Synod had been questioned. The Reverend Eric Norelius, pastor of the congregations at Vasa and Red Wing, noted that "English missions" had begun to attract Minnesota Swedes away from the Augustana churches.

Though he launched a campaign that led to a gradual transition to English, the change took many years. Synod minutes were not available in an English version until 1919. In 1921, even after the bitter attacks on foreign-language use fostered by World War I, 85% of all sermons in synod churches were reportedly in Swedish. The first complete English order of service was not drawn up until 1925.

Nils Hasselmo, a Minnesota scholar who studied the use of Swedish in the Chisago Lakes community, found that before 1915 all church activities were conducted in Swedish and all records were in Swedish. By the middle 1920s occasional English services were held, Sunday school classes were conducted in both Swedish and English, and summer "Swede schools" were still offered. A decade later English and Swedish services were held regularly, Sunday school classes were principally in English, and the summer language schools were no more. By 1945 all regular services were conducted in English, and the language transition was complete.

The demise of the Swedish language in America did not occur without protest. Many Swedes felt that there was a close connection between their language and their religion. As scholars of the language transition have pointed out, "They had received their religious upbringing by reading the *Bible* in Swedish, by memorizing their catechism in Swedish, and by attending services in Swedish. For many it was difficult to translate their faith into English." As late as 1931, the pastor of the Chisago Lakes church cautioned, "This community is an ultra-Swedish [*ultrasvenskt*] one. Therefore, we do not wish to speed up an inappropriate Americanization and thereby harm the sensitive plant of the spiritual life. We ought to move cautiously in these sacred areas."

Gradually, however, the Swedish language in Minnesota died. One scholar estimated that the largest number of Minnesotans ever to have some knowledge of Swedish

Bible verses in Swedish adorned the front of the Almelund Lutheran Church in Chisago County, about 1910.

was about 300,000, or 15% of the state's population, just before World War I. The 1970 census enumerated 105,472 Minnesotans who spoke Swedish, nearly half of whom lived in the seven-county Twin Cities metropolitan area. By then Swedish as a second language was used more to exchange pleasantries and as a badge of the speakers' Swedishness than as language used for everyday conversation.

With the passing of the first generation, it seems likely that the Swedish language lost its function as a primary means of communication, except in areas like Chisago County, where the density of Swedish Americans was so great that few daily conversations were likely to take place with members of any other national group. Some visitors from a rural Småland parish observed as late as 1963 that a German used-car salesman in that county could also speak the Småland dialect, claiming that he would not be able to sell cars there if he could not. Even in 1980, some third-generation Swedish Americans there could speak the Småland dialect. Conditions changed between the 1960s and the 1980s as the area became popular with commuters, and the influence of television made itself increasingly felt.[30]

In 2003 Swedish was taught for academic credit at the University of Minnesota, Gustavus Adolphus College, Bethel College, and Sjölunden, one of the Concordia College language villages, and noncredit classes were offered at the American Swedish Institute in Minneapolis and at various other venues, including *Svenska Skolan,* a Saturday session for young children. A native of Sweden who taught 14 of the 20 language classes at the American Swedish Institute said the number of students had doubled in the years since 1980. Classes were a mixture of older and younger students, who usually had some Swedish connection.[31]

Churches

Most Swedish immigrants in the 19th century belonged to the Lutheran church, which was the state church of Sweden, but others had joined the Baptists, Methodists, and Mormons or evangelical reform movements within the Lutheran church. While immigrants could have affiliated with English-speaking churches in America whose doctrines were compatible with their own beliefs, many chose not to do so.

Although they received no help or encouragement from the church at home, one of the first things many Swedish

Programs such as Time Travel encourage children to try living as their ancestors did. Each youngster dresses in pioneer garb and learns about the foods, chores, and games of a long-ago childhood. McKay Siverhus coped with the vagaries of frying bacon on a wood-burning stove in a 2002 program.

settlers in Minnesota did was to establish Lutheran congregations in their new communities. There were congregations in St. Paul, Center City, Scandia, Vasa, and Red Wing by 1855 and seven more by 1858, when the Minnesota Conference was founded. It was originally affiliated with the Northern Illinois synod, which included Norwegians, Germans, and Americans. The two Scandinavian groups withdrew in 1860 to establish the Scandinavian Lutheran Augustana Synod but parted ways in 1870, and

Women from the Salem Evangelical Lutheran Church (later the Stockholm Lutheran Church) took a break from their activities, probably serving at a district meeting, about 1910. Most wore their best lace-trimmed aprons, but the two women on the left were likely kitchen workers, judging from their darker aprons. Women such as these were the backbone of many Lutheran church activities.

Augustana became an exclusively Swedish American Lutheran body.

Some immigrant members of the Mission Friends, a pietist movement within the Lutheran church in Sweden, were not comfortable in the Augustana Synod, and they founded two Mission synods, which merged to form the Swedish Evangelical Mission Covenant of America in 1885. By 1906, Minnesota had 80 Mission Covenant congregations, with a membership of 5,017, making the Mission Covenant group the second largest Swedish church body in the state but far smaller than Augustana.

Swedish pietists who belonged to Baptist and Methodist churches in Sweden were able to continue their affiliation after emigration. In Minnesota the Baptists outnumbered the Methodists; there were 49 congregations with a membership of 3,542 by 1892. In both churches Swedish congregations were given considerable control over their own affairs through membership in special Swedish conferences.

Missionary work among Swedish immigrants by the Yankee Congregationalists yielded few converts. The church's high social prestige did not make it attractive to a foreign immigrant population, and none of the approximately two dozen Swedish Congregational churches established in Minnesota between 1880 and 1920 existed by 1950. Two other Protestant denominations, Presbyterian and Episcopal, carried on mission work among the Swedes in Minnesota. The Episcopalians were more successful than the Presbyterians, and by 1910 there were eight Swedish Episcopal churches in the state.

Churches other than Lutheran seemed to have made the transition from Swedish to English at a rate similar to the Lutherans. In 1928 Swedish Methodists lost their separate identity, and about the same time Swedish Baptist congregations began gradually to Americanize. In 1945 the term "Swedish" was dropped from the Baptist conference title. English became the official language of the Swedish Evangelical Mission Covenant Church in 1929, and it became known simply as the Evangelical Covenant Church. Even the Swedish origins of the Augustana Synod were submerged when it joined three other groups in 1962 to form the Lutheran Church in America (LCA). The LCA, the American Lutheran Church, and the Association of Evangelical Lutheran Churches merged in 1987 to form the Evangelical Lutheran Church in America.

After World War II, Swedish Americans were well integrated into American religious life, although many congregations still honored their Swedish beginnings. In a few congregations, such as Augustana Church in Minneapolis, the traditional *Julotta* continued to be held early on Christmas morning. Others put on annual events reflecting their Swedish heritage. But they are a celebration of the past, not a part of early 21st-century reality. A hundred years after the first Swedish settlers reached Minnesota religious assimilation had become a fact.[32]

Many of the early churches also functioned as de facto social service agencies. Eric Norelius founded the Vasa Children's Home in Vasa when his congregation took in four orphaned children of Swedish immigrants. Other churches, such as First Lutheran in St. Paul and Augustana in Minneapolis were instrumental in starting hospitals

The children's home in Vasa founded by Pastor Norelius in 1865 occupied several structures over the years. This building replaced one that was demolished in a tornado in 1879. The charitable work begun with this home eventually developed into the Lutheran Social Services.

Student nurses practiced meal preparation in the diet kitchen of Swedish Hospital in Minneapolis in 1917. The hospital was established in 1898, and the School of Nursing followed a year later. Initially the school required young women to be able to speak both English and Swedish because most of the medical staff and the patients were Swedish. First Lutheran Church in St. Paul was instrumental in building Bethesda Hospital for Swedish-speaking patients in 1892.

and homes for the elderly. Often it was the women, such as the members of Women's Missionary Society of Augustana Synod, later known as the Women of the Evangelical Lutheran Church in America, who did most of the social outreach.[33]

Ruth Youngdahl Nelson was one of these church ladies. Nelson, who married a Lutheran pastor, wrote many books affirming her faith and was also active in causes. She was arrested on August 14, 1982, for protesting against the first Trident nuclear submarine, but the charges were later dropped. Her remarkable family included her brothers, Pastor Reuben Youngdahl, who built the congregation of

Mount Olivet Lutheran Church in south Minneapolis from 331 souls to 10,000 at the time of his death, making it the largest Lutheran congregation in the U.S., and Minnesota Governor and Judge Luther W. Youngdahl.[34]

Social action was not just a province of the churches. In 1904, a group of Swedish and Swedish American women founded the Linnea Society. Through dues collected at monthly meetings and fund-raisers such as dinners and ice cream socials, the ladies—with the help of some generous contributions—opened the Linnea Home for the elderly in 1917. Then next year they held a linen shower to furnish it. The home, at 2040 Como Avenue in St. Paul, housed 71 people in 2003.[35]

Civic Assimilation

As the Swedes became part of the larger community, they began to take an active part in government. Hans Mattson, elected secretary of state in Minnesota in 1869, was the first Swedish immigrant to be elected to a state office, and he led the way for what became a string of federal, state, and local office holders. Some have even argued that candidates with Scandinavian surnames stand a better chance of being elected.[36]

Many Minnesota governors have been Swedish immigrants or descendants of immigrants, from John Lind to Wendell Anderson and Arne Carlson. Among those between Lind and Carlson was the popular John A. Johnson, son of a Swedish immigrant, who was elected in 1904 and was being mentioned as a candidate for president when he died in office in 1909. During the 12 hours that he lay in state in state capital rotunda on September 22, approximately 75,000 mourners filed past. Johnson, a Democrat, was succeeded by his lieutenant governor, the Republican Albert O. Eberhart, a Swedish immigrant who came alone to the U.S. at the age of 11 to join his family.[37]

A 1908 postcard promoting Governor John A. Johnson as a presidential candidate featured a union message and was sponsored by the Veterans of '62 United in Defense of the Flag.

The first real test of civic assimilation for Swedish Americans came during World War I, when there was unprecedented pressure on ethnic Americans to reject their native culture. The Scandinavians were watched closely, though the situation was far worse for German Americans. As the war began, Swedish Americans openly expressed sympathy for the Central Powers. On July 22, 1914, an article in *Svenska Amerikanska Posten* stated that the brewing crisis was just another example of the classic Germanic-Slavic struggle. Russia, Sweden's traditional enemy, was viewed as the villain, and the plight of Finland, under Russian rule for a century, was pointed out. On August 12, after Sweden and Norway jointly declared neutrality, *Posten* editor wrote that Sweden might yet side with the Germans, noting that if the German people lost, the cost would be enormous, for the conflict was a holy war, an effort by "Greek Catholicism" to dominate the world.

Although only a minority of Swedish-language newspapers in the United States whole-heartedly supported Germany, evidence from *Veckobladet* and *Minnesota Stats Tidning* as well as from *Svenska Amerikanska Posten* suggests that there was considerable pro-German feeling within the Minnesota Swedish community, especially in Minneapolis, in 1914. As German submarines became more active in the Atlantic in 1916, the Swedish American press pleaded almost unanimously for America to stay neutral. As late as February 14, 1917, *Posten* urged bipartisan support for President Woodrow Wilson's policy against Germany while expressing hope that the United States would not enter the war.

Many of Minnesota's prominent Swedish American elected officials echoed the early pro-German and later neutrality stances of the press. Most vocally antiwar were Congressmen Charles A. Lindbergh, Sr., (father of the famed aviator) and Ernest Lundeen. During the debate over American entry on the House floor, Lundeen stated that the American people did not want war and insisted that war should not be declared without a national plebiscite. He reported that an incomplete poll of his 54,000 constituents showed them 10 to 1 against entry. Lindbergh opposed American involvement on the grounds that the war would benefit "professional speculators" and "'the lords of special privilege' who 'in their selfish glee [were] coining billions of profit from the rage of war.'"[38]

Twenty years later, Lindbergh's son Charles, who was probably the nation's first superhero after his solo flight from the United States to France in 1927, voiced strong public opposition to the United States entering World War II. His wife, Anne Morrow Lindbergh, saw this as a link to his father's earlier stand. A. Scott Berg, in his biography of Lindbergh, quoted a letter she wrote to her mother-in-law:

Charles A. Lindbergh, Sr. (left), served in Congress from 1907 to 1917, and Ernest Lundeen (right) from 1917 to 1919. They faced such anti-Swedish propaganda as a business-card handout that said: "Vote for—Hindenburg, Lindenburg, Lundeenburg, And Let's All Go To Hell Together."

"Won't it be strange if Charles will be fighting the same fight as his father, years ago!"[39]

When Congress declared war in April 1917, public expressions of antiwar opinion by Swedish Americans in Minnesota ceased. On May 9, 1917, *Posten* blamed Kaiser Wilhelm for starting the war and called for his abdication so that peace could be made with a democratic Germany. Meanwhile some Minnesota political leaders of Swedish descent campaigned to rally Swedish American opinion to the cause. Traveling through the state to promote draft registration, former Governor John Lind, a native of Sweden, emphasized that no single nation was totally responsible for starting the war, but he asked listeners to consider how long it would "be before they dominate us" if the

John Lind, who was born in Kanna, Sweden in 1854, served in the U.S. House of Representatives, 1887–93, and as governor of Minnesota, 1899–1901. In 1913 he was the personal representative of President Woodrow Wilson to Mexico.

Prussians take over Europe. "This is a just war and a holy war," he said, "And to the young people who will take part in it I say, 'God be with you for you are the protectors of humanity.'"

Resistance to the draft was not uncommon among recent immigrants. They had left a country in which rapid industrialization was bringing increasing social reform. The worldwide Socialist movement was far more appealing for them than it had been for those who left Sweden 50 or 60 years earlier. In Minnesota the members of the Commission of Public Safety, created in 1917, knew that many Swedes and other Scandinavians opposed the war, and the commission had virtually dictatorial powers to distribute prowar propaganda and to restrict activities it considered hostile. The commission tried to approach leading members of ethnic groups whose loyalty might be doubted and enlist their help in planning an "educational campaign."

The commission hired agents to attend rallies and meetings around the state and relay any information they gathered about the activities of "foreigners," "radicals," "slackers," and any others suspected of lack of enthusiasm for the war. A letter dated May 31, 1917, and headed "C. H.

reports," told of a visit to the shoe repair shop of a man he described as a known German Socialist, who purportedly said "that a good many are against conscription, especially among the socialists; that if the socialists refuse to register, he believes many of this number will be Swedes, and that this is because they do not like Russia and the socialist movement is strong among the Swedes; and the fact that Russia is an old enemy of Sweden, would tend to keep them from registering. . . . I judge from what he said that they are using this argument about Russia, in an effort to influence the Swedes against enlisting."

Two agents were apparently assigned to investigate the activities of supposed Socialists among the Swedes of Chisago County in June. They found a local informant who identified some Socialists "who are stirring up the people of that locality to such an extent that he is afraid they will cause considerable trouble." The agents reported hearsay evidence of several Socialist meetings, naming the supposed ringleaders and stating that "the people who attended the meeting . . . were all Swedish Lutherans" except one, who was a German. The informant told one agent that several farmers refused to buy Liberty Bonds and concluded that this meant they were Socialists. He told the agent that he "hoped the Governor would inform these men . . . that their views were known to him and that any attempt on their part to agitate the people against the Government in this crisis would cause them severe punishment. This he felt would put a stop to this socialism, which he felt is at present growing hourly . . . and would 'blot out the stain now placed on the fair name of the Swedish people of this community.'"

When World War II broke out, Minnesota felt no need to establish another Public Safety Commission. In 20 years the supposed threat of the hyphenated Swede had diminished.[40]

Swedish-Oriented Organizations

Although the churches were very important to many Swedish immigrants, perhaps fewer than half of the immigrants belonged to a church. Many of the other Swedes in Minnesota found ethnic homes in a variety of secular organizations. They were particularly important in the major urban areas where large concentrations of people ensured a wide variety of interests and church membership was low. The aims of these organizations ranged from moral missions in the case of the International Order of Good Templars temperance lodges, through the provision of insurance benefits in mutual aid societies such as the Vasa Order of America, the Norden Society, *Svenska Brö-*

Several lodges convened for the annual meeting of the International Order of Good Templars in Hallock, Kittson County, in June 1908.

derna (the Swedish Brothers), and the Gustavus II Adolphus Society.[41] The Swedish Brothers—who had their own building and their own song—and Norden were organized as early as the late 1860s, but the bulk seem to have appeared during the three decades preceding World War I. Their flourishing numbers show that Swedes, even in the cities, possessed a vigorous sense of ethnicity at that time.

The disruptive influence of World War I was also felt by secular organizations. Interest waned in the 1920s as the older generations persisted in using a language the young did not understand, and by the end of the decade the ethnic club appeared to be out of date. In the 1930s, however, Swedish secular organizations received renewed attention, stimulated in part by the Great Depression. But the effects of the Depression were mixed. Some argue that the unprecedented hard times hastened assimilation while at the same time pushing Swedes and other national groups to band together for security in a trying time. The banding together may suggest that the ties still held in spite of the progress assimilation had made, or it may be seen as a reaction against this assimilation. Action was needed to keep memories of the homeland and its culture from fading forever.[42] By 2003 several of these groups remained active, including ones such as *Dalaföreningen, Värmlandsförbundet,* and *Västergötland* Society, which are aimed at those who have a connection with specific provinces in Sweden.

The most notable organization to arise in Minnesota during the first third of the 20th century was the American Swedish Institute. Seventy-five years after its founding, it continued to be a rallying point for Swedish Americans in Minnesota. In mid-2003, there were more than 6,000 member households, in all 50 states and several countries, and that number was growing steadily. Its collection and program needs have prompted plans for a building adjacent to the 33-room Turnblad mansion housing the Institute.

The American Swedish Institute in 1935

The American Swedish Institute is regarded by many as one of the leading ethnic-specific museums and cultural centers in the United States. Even at its inception, its functions were different from those of the clubs and societies of the early 20th century. Then such organizations were essential to the well-being of their members, often providing the only place where urban Swedish Americans could find companionship. They were the institutions of a truly ethnic society. Although the institute, then and now, also has provided camaraderie, it serves multiple purposes for its

Young women processed down the stairs at the American Swedish Institute for a Santa Lucia ceremony in 1951.

A couple in folk dress demonstrated a traditional dance on the grounds of the American Swedish Institute.

members and visitors in the 21th century—from educating Swedish-Americans about their past to providing a forum presenting various aspects of contemporary Sweden and Swedish America to serving as a link between immigrants of different origins and generations.

In recent years, artists from Sweden and from Swedish America have exhibited at the Institute, and its tradition of promoting Swedish crafts is flourishing. For the past several years, provincial fairs, from different Swedish provinces, have showcased both traditional and contemporary arts and crafts.[43]

Swedish culture continues to be preserved by other groups. Many, such as choral, dance, drama, and instrumental clubs or troupes, are dedicated to the arts. One is the *Nyckelharpalag*, formed in 1998 to play traditional Swedish music, primarily from the Uppland region of Sweden, on a keyed fiddle.[44] In addition, there are annual festivals of Scandinavian films and contemporary music in the Twin Cities. Also, both Swedish Americans and natives of Sweden are active in the Minnesota chapter of the Swedish-American Chamber of Commerce. Those interested in delving into their Swedish heritage gravitate to the Swedish American Genealogy Society. Many groups, both in the Twin Cities and in other areas of Minnesota, focus on some aspect of Swedish heritage and culture or meet for social reasons.

Efforts to celebrate Swedish heritage in Minnesota are long-standing. Probably the first such occasion was the commemoration of the 250th anniversary of Swedish immigration to America. Hans Mattson was one of the organizers of the event, which was held at an exposition building in Minneapolis on September 14, 1888. The three-hour program drew 15,000 attendees, but the parade had to be cancelled due to rain.[45]

Organizations such as the American Swedish Institute, joined by smaller groups, keep memories of the Swedish

Flickorna Fem (The Five Girls) is dedicated to performing Swedish and Swedish American songs. Nina Clark, Christine Albertsson, Elisabeth Skoglund, Malla Corbett, and Carline Bengtsson (left to right) are fluent in Swedish and either natives of Sweden or of Swedish descent or married to a Swede.

heritage alive. The Swedish Council of America, headquartered in Minneapolis, serves as an umbrella group for these and other Swedish American societies and institutions nationally. In 1933, only a few years after immigration peaked, the first *Svenskarnas Dag* celebration was held in Minnehaha Park near the large Scandinavian neighborhood in South Minneapolis. Earlier celebrations had been held at Phalen Park in St. Paul. *Svenskarnas Dag*, held close to the date of the traditional Swedish Midsummer Day festival, became an annual event and continues to attract celebrants, though their numbers have dwindled.[46]

It seems appropriate that Scandia, briefly the home of the first Swedish settlers, is the location of *Gammelgården* (The Old Farm), a collection of buildings, most of which date from the early Swedish pioneer era. They include an immigrant house, the 1856 first structure of Elim Lutheran

This group enjoyed good weather for the Svenskarnas Dag celebration at Minnehaha Park in Minneapolis in 1955.

Church, the first parsonage for the church, built in 1868, a barn from about 1879, and a *stuga,* or vacation house, built in the 1930s, plus a new visitor center. The presence of the open-air museum, the only one of its kind devoted to Swedish settlers in the country according to the director Lynne Blomstrand Moratzka, is announced by the Swedish-style rail fence. *Gammelgården* was founded in 1972.[47]

By 2000 numerous local festivals emphasizing cultural origins had sprung up in Minnesota towns where Swedish settlement was important. Many of them, such as *Svenskarnas Dag,* were tied to ones in Sweden. Others, such as *Nisswa-stämman,* which drew together musicians and dancers, celebrated aspects of Swedish American culture.

In Lindstrom, Karl Oskar Days were named for the main
character in the Moberg novels about immigration. At Old
Mill State Park in Marshall County, the mill, established by
Swedish immigrants, once again produced whole-wheat
flour on one grinding day a year.[48]

Along with Swedish Minnesotans' curiosity about their
heritage was a growing fascination about the emigration of
their ancestors to America and particularly to Minnesota.
Novelist Vilhelm Moberg's saga about Karl Oskar Nilsson
and his Swedish family's flight from poverty and hunger to

The Moberg Mystique

Vilhelm Moberg would be surprised to find that his fictional characters have developed a virtual life of their own in Lindstrom in Chisago County. Moberg researched his saga about Swedish immigrants by visiting Lindstrom and the surrounding area in 1948. The four best-selling novels that resulted—*The Emigrants, Unto a Good Land, The Settlers,* and *The Last Letter Home*—were made into two films starring Liv Ullman and Max Von Sydow. The books are greatly loved in Sweden, and many Swedish visitors and others are drawn to Lindstrom because of them. A few visitors have believed that Kristina and Karl Oskar were real people and asked where they had lived and where they were buried. Eventually, the community put up statues of the couple and later renovated a house several miles south of Lindstrom in which a real immigrant family had lived. The house is called *Nya Duvemåla* after Kristina's fictional Swedish home. It is meticulously restored and includes such features as hand-crocheted curtains, made by a volunteer who used her grandmother's old Swedish pattern. About a thousand people—90% of them from Sweden—visit the house annually.

The Moberg connection continued when two members of the Swedish pop group ABBA—composer Benny Andersson and lyricist Björn Ulvaeus—wrote *Kristina från Duvemåla,* a musical based on the Moberg books. It was performed first in Sweden and later, in 1996, in Minneapolis and at Chisago Lakes High School in Lindstrom.

Nya Duvemåla, a restored immigrant house in Lindstrom. The large rock supporting the flags of the United States, Minnesota, and Sweden was imported from Sweden.

Skiers raced to the finish line in 2003 in the annual Mora Vasaloppet. Each year in February skiers converge on this town, named for a Swedish immigrant's home in Dalarna, to compete in a variety of races for both adults and children. The winner of the 58 K race received a trip to the Vasaloppet in Sweden.

a new life on the shores of Chisago Lake and the two full-length films based on it did much to fan the flames of interest.[49]

In 1965 the Swedish Emigrant Institute was founded in Växjö, Sweden, in the heart of one of the earliest areas of emigration. Three years later the institute held a celebration called Minnesota Day in an adjoining park. It has been held annually ever since. The Växjö museum has become a mecca for Swedish Americans visiting the Old Country.

Symbolic of the ties between Minnesota and Sweden is the recognition that five Minnesotans have received by being named Swedish-American of the Year by the king and queen of Sweden. In 2003 this honor went to Marilyn Carlson Nelson, the chief executive officer of Carlson Companies, a corporation founded by her father who received the award in 1981. Governors Wendell Anderson and Arne Carlson and University of Minnesota president Nils Hasselmo were recognized in earlier years. The increased exchange of visitors and ideas between Minnesota and Sweden over the past four decades has helped to make people much more aware of the lasting impact Swedish immigrants have had on Minnesota's culture.[50]

It is not just the bountiful smörgåsbord shared by Swedish Minnesotans at Christmas that marks Minnesota as the most Swedish of all states. The Swedish immigrants added their distinct flavor to both public and private facets of state society. They would be pleased to know that many of their descendants are celebrating their ancestral culture by a lively interest in exploring their roots and traditions.

Personal Account:
Memories from a Stay in the United States
by Evelina Månsson

Evelina Månsson wrote her memoirs in Swedish of her six years in Minnesota in 1930 after she returned to Sweden for good. She first came to the United States in 1901, traveling third class on the steamer Campania. *Talkative and ambitious, she had adventures from the moment she reached New York:*

"Every immigrant had to possess twenty-five dollars. I didn't own twenty-five dollars, but a relative in whose company I was traveling succeeded ... in smuggling the amount to me, which I thus had until the ceremony was over."

When she arrived in Minnesota, older immigrants peppered her with questions about Sweden:

"Oh, they mostly thought that Swedish conditions were the same as when they left Sweden almost thirty years ago, and they hardly wanted to believe me when I described conditions as they were now."

Evelina was anxious to get work, although her uncle thought she had plenty of time:

"But I didn't think so. I was burning with impatience for the opportunity to earn a little money so that I could at least pay my debts. You see, I was in debt for most of my ticket. I started out in America burdened with debt, which was certainly very common. . . . Finally my uncle came home from town one day and announced that he had managed to find me a good place. The next morning I . . . started work in America as a servant girl in Hector."

Her employers, a couple with five children, were Swedish American, but most of the conversation was in English. That, and her own restlessness and ambition, made her leave the post for Minneapolis, despite the job's advantages:

"Everything went precisely and punctually in the house where I was in service. Everything in its appointed place at its appointed time; no cheating or sloppiness. Every day of the week and every hour of the day had its special task. . . . On Monday we did the wash. . . . On Tuesday the whole wash was ironed. . . . On Wednesday the upstairs was cleaned. . . . On

Evelina Johansdotter Månsson (right) and her sister Augusta, Minneapolis, about 1905

Thursday there was no extra work as the idea was that the maid would have the afternoon off. On Friday afternoon chickens were plucked for the family's use and for Mrs. Petterson's sister, who didn't have a maid. . . .On Saturday all the bread for the week was baked. . . . Sunday should have been a day of rest, but a maid didn't get much of that."

"I ended up very well off—decent people, kind treatment, reasonable work, tolerable pay—what more could I need as a maid! And yet, one does not live by bread alone. . . . I had no one to communicate with. . . . And since I had very few acquaintances and consequently few visitors and I seldom read newspapers—there was no newspaper in Swedish in this home—I was very ignorant about what took place out in the world. When the family was gathered . . . English was always spoken, of which I understood nothing and therefore the news from town was a secret to me. . . . I knew nothing, learned nothing and didn't dare ask about anything, and I was boundlessly interested in everything. No, it was unendurable! I decided to resign my position and travel to Minneapolis, where I knew some girls from Sweden. Maybe in such a big city there would be some other kind of work, which offered a little more freedom, a little more happiness than could be found within a kitchen's narrow walls. . . . Two weeks after this decision I was ready to set off on the journey to Minneapolis."

Evelina found her friends, but the job they had told her about—at a laundry— had been filled. So she embarked on a series of disastrous jobs until she found one that suited her. Her first attempt was at a boardinghouse, on Fifth Avenue South:

"There were three girls employed there—a Swede, a Norwegian and one of another nationality. The Swedish one was sick and left as soon as I came, for I was to take over her job, which consisted of washing dishes, scrubbing floors, etc. Someone loaned me a kitchen apron, and I set to work right away. . . . After standing at the dishpan three full hours straight, I finally got dinner, which was laid out any which way on a kitchen table still cluttered with dirty dishes. It was excellent food, but it had cooled off, and besides I had no appetite. . . . I started to wonder whether I would really like it in this place. . . . After finishing my work in the kitchen, I was to wash the floors in the dining rooms. . . . When I was done with this work, the first guests for supper began to arrive, and three hours at the dish pan beckoned all over again. But I could manage without them. . . . I took off the kitchen apron, went up to the Norwegian girl's room and asked her to say to 'the mistress' that I did not think I was suited to the job, but aimed to leave right away."

And so, her job search started all over again.

"I went out and bought myself an *Evening Tribune*. There were hundreds of jobs of all possible kinds. What did I dare try? 'Swedish girl wanted for household of three persons,' I read. Perhaps this was something for me!"

She got the job, working for an old couple and their adult son, Pete, whose wife had died. The work was much easier than in Hector and for three weeks, all went well. Then she noticed a change in the woman's attitude toward her and discovered:

"She thought I was after her Pete! No, thanks . . . her unfounded suspicions spoiled everything for me. . . . I resigned my position and moved within a week."

Evelina stayed with a friend for a couple of weeks while she was looking for yet another job:

"There was no job I thought I would like, even though there were hundreds of jobs of all possible types. . . . There were positions as maid for working families, or in shops or for shopkeepers and tavern keepers, and so on, but none of them were attractive to me."

Finally she took a job in a sewing factory:

"I . . . showed up there in the morning to sew. . . . I was assigned to a machine along with a bundle of cut-out shirts. . . . Then I was supposed to sew, but I had no idea how to operate the machine and no one seemed to have time to teach me . . . so I spent the morning looking around and doing nothing. When the noon break came, many girls went out to eat dinner and I . . . went out too, not to eat but directly home with the feeling I had been as much of a sewing girl as I was going to be."

After brief stints in a laundry, where Evelina managed to sneak out when her washing machine went berserk, and another private home, she tagged along with a friend to a job interview and there she found her dream job:

"[Josefina] was going to the Guaranty Loan Building to come to an agreement about a job as cleaning woman there. . . . I decided to go with her; it would be interesting to see how it looked inside such a big building."

The head janitor, also a Swede, hired both girls, and Evelina was thrilled:

"Guaranty Loan Building was Minneapolis' highest and perhaps even largest office building. . . . Its twelve stories were 172 feet high, with an observation tower fifty feet higher yet, and the building housed 400 offices. It was situated . . . on the corner of Third Street and Second Avenue South. . . . In this building, a little city in itself, I would be working! How happy I was about this unexpected change in my situation. . . . I would avoid staying shut up in a hot kitchen for days on end; yes, I would also avoid working at a laundry. . . . I would work mornings and evenings and when the sun burned hottest I would be able to sit and enjoy myself in Riverside Park!"

Things went well on the job, but English still baffled Evelina:

"When the office gentlemen spoke to me to give some sort of instruction about the work, or perhaps they were talking about something completely different . . . I nodded understandingly and pretended to grasp precisely what they wanted and they looked satisfied and went away, while I set about my work again, not a bit wiser than I had been, but amused to my heart's content over the comical situation."

Evelina took stock of her progress after she had been in America for one year, the "dog year," as she called it:

"I had completely paid for my ticket, bought my furniture with cash, and bought all the clothes I needed for the time being. . . . Thus I had come so far along that I could begin to save a little money. . . . After a year and a half's stay in America I sent for my sister from Sweden. . . . When she arrived, I got her work right away at Guaranty Loan."

Life was not just work for the sisters. They went to the Minnesota State Fair, the circus, musical evenings, and lectures. Evelina had saved enough money to return to Sweden after three and one-half years. She returned to Minnesota again, and once again tried her luck in a sewing factory, where she managed to sew through her finger. Eventually she married, and the couple returned to Sweden, where she lived out her life. Her description of leaving America the first time captures her ambivalence about returning to Sweden:

"It was with indescribable feelings that I took leave of the country to which I once came as a poor foreigner, but where I was well-received and so I left that day with my heart overflowing with gratitude and regret."

Source: Evelina Månsson, "Amerika-minnen: Upplevelser och iakttagelser från en 6-årig vistelse i U.S.A." (America Memories: Experiences and Observations from a 6-year stay in the U.S.A.), 1930, MHS, translated by Carolyn Anderson, with additional translating and editing by Anne Gillespie Lewis.

For Further Reading

Anderson, Philip J., and Dag Blanck, eds., *Swedes in the Twin Cities: Immigrant Life and Minnesota's Urban Frontier.* St. Paul: Minnesota Historical Society Press, 2001.

Holmquist, June D., ed. *They Chose Minnesota: A Survey of the State's Ethnic Groups.* St. Paul: Minnesota Historical Society Press, 1981.

Johnson, Emeroy. *Eric Norelius, Pioneer Midwest Pastor and Churchman.* Rock Island, Illinois: published in cooperation with the Minnesota Conference of the Augustana Lutheran Church, Augustana Book Concern, 1954.

Lewis, Anne Gillespie. *The American Swedish Institute: Turnblad's Castle.* Minneapolis: American Swedish Institute, 1999.

———. *So Far Away in the World: Stories from the Swedish Twin Cities.* Minneapolis: Nodin Press, 2002.

Mattson, Hans. *Reminiscences, The Story of an Emigrant.* St. Paul: D. D. Merrill Company, 1891. (First published in Swedish in 1890.)

Moberg, Vilhelm, *The Emigrants, The Last Letter Home, The Settlers,* and *Unto a Good Land.* St. Paul: Minnesota Historical Society Press, 1995. (First published in Swedish in 1949, 1952, 1956, and 1959.)

Nordstrom, Byron, ed., *The Swedes in Minnesota.* Minneapolis: T. S. Denison and Co., 1976.

Norelius, Eric. *Early Life of Eric Norelius, (1833-1862)—A Lutheran Pioneer. His Own Story Rendered into English by Emeroy Johnson.* Rock Island, Illinois: Augustana Book Concern, 1934.

Strand, A[lgot] E., ed., *History of the Swedish-Americans of Minnesota,* 3 vols. Chicago: The Lewis Publishing Co., 1910.

Notes

1. Although this remark may strike a chord with many Swedish Americans in Minnesota, who probably made many similar comments on Christmas Eve, it was uttered by Ben Post of Lindstrom in 2001 and repeated to the author by Linda Gronvall, his aunt, on Jan. 22, 2003.

2. All information on the 2000 Census is available from the Census website: www.census.gov. Statistics regarding Minnesota and California respondents declaring their Swedish ancestry (and percentages) are from Summary File 3, Quick Tables, located by clicking on American FactFinder on the Census site and selecting the Ancestry table within the Social Characteristics field, with the respective states selected as the geographic areas. Information showing ranking among U.S. counties and also cities of more than 5,000 is from E. Marie Pees of the Bureau of the Census, using Census 2000 Summary File 3, Tables PCT16 and PCT17.

3. Author's conversation with Gloria Swanson, Hallock, fall 2003.

4. The statistics on Minnesota in the 1990 Census are on the U.S. Census website and in bound copies in various agencies, including the Minnesota Historical Society (hereafter MHS), St. Paul. The 1990 ancestry information is from Table 31 of the Social and Economic Characteristics section.

5. John G. Rice, "The Swedes," in *They Chose Minnesota: A Survey of the State's Ethnic Groups,* ed. June Drenning Holmquist (St. Paul: Minnesota Historical Society Press, 1981), 248.

6. Eric Norelius, *Early Life of Eric Norelius (1833–1862): Lutheran Pioneer,* trans.

Emeroy Johnson (Rock Island: Augustana Book Concern, 1934), 74–76, 103. At the time of the greatest immigration, Swedes took their father's first name, plus the designation "son" or "dotter" (daughter) to form their last names. Thus a son of Anders became Andersson. On arrival in the U.S., many of the immigrants dropped the second "s." Therefore, as in this passage, names may be given both with and without the double "s." Rice, "The Swedes," 249.

7. Rice, "The Swedes," 252.

8. Norelius, *Early Life of Eric Norelius,* 272.

9. For preceding two paragraphs, see Rice, "The Swedes," 253.

10. Rice, "The Swedes," 253–54.

11. For preceding two paragraphs, see Rice, "The Swedes," 254.

12. For the preceding seven paragraphs, see Rice, "The Swedes," 249, 254, 258.

13. For the preceding two paragraphs, see Rice, "The Swedes," 258. See also Hans Mattson, *Reminiscences: The Story of an Emigrant* (St. Paul: D. D. Merrill Co., 1891), first published in Swedish as *Minnen* (Lund: C. W. K. Gleerup, 1890). Dr. Wesley J. Matson, a relative of Mattson, provided the author with background material.

14. For the preceding two paragraphs, see Rice, "The Swedes," 258.

15. Rice, "The Swedes," 260.

16. Author's conversation with Bud Erickson, winter 2003.

17. Kittson County Historical Society and the Red River Valley Historical Society, comps., *Our Northwest Corner: Histories of Kittson County, Minnesota* (Dallas: Taylor Pub. Co., 1976), 43.

18. For the preceding three paragraphs, see Rice, "The Swedes," 260.

19. For the preceding three paragraphs, see Rice, "The Swedes," 260–61.

20. For the preceding four paragraphs, see Rice, "The Swedes," 260–62. For a discussion of textile workers, see Lars Olsson, "Evelina Johansdotter, Textile Workers, and the Musingwear Family: Class, Gender, and Ethnicity in the Political Economy of Minnesota at the end of World War I," in *Swedes in the Twin Cities: Immigrant Life and Minnesota's Urban Frontier,* ed. Philip J. Anderson and Dag Blanck (St. Paul: Minnesota Historical Society Press, 2001), 77–90.

21. For the Twin Cities, see Rice, "The Swedes," 262–64; Norelius, *Early Life of Eric Norelius,* 300–301 (quote). See also, David A. Lanegren, "Swedish Neighborhoods of the Twin Cities: From Swede Hollow to Arlington Hills, From Snoose Boulevard to Minnehaha Parkway," in *Swedes in the Twin Cities,* 39–56; Anne Gillespie Lewis, *So Far Away in the World: Stories from the Swedish Twin Cities,* (Minneapolis: Nodin Press, 2002) 83 (quote), 14.

22. Rice, "The Swedes," 264.

23. For an account of Turnblad's travels, see Anne Gillespie Lewis, *The American Swedish Institute: Turnblad's Castle* (Minneapolis: American Swedish Institute, 1999), 21–24; for examples of letters to Sweden, see the letters of John Wallberg in Lewis, *So Far Away in the World,* 43–45; William Carlson, Signe Olson Peterson's grandson, provided information about her to the author; people in Sweden—even those who were born long after local residents emigrated—knew about them, as illustrated by a remark made by a young man about the late Emil Wallin of Isanti during a visit to Sweden in 1978, fifty-one years after Wallin left, and overheard and repeated to the author by his daughter, Marlys Wallin Wickstrom: "It's about time Emil came home again."

24. Rice, "The Swedes," 265.

25. The author, who is of Scandinavian heritage, grew up in the heavily Swedish American neighborhood of Camden in north Minneapolis and heard many remarks to this effect then and in later years. See Nils and Patricia Hasselmo, "American Swedish Revisited," in *Swedes in the Twin Cities,* 240–50, for an illuminating and amusing essay on language.

26. Rice, "The Swedes," 265.

27. Author's conversation with Lawrence Hammerstrom, Eagan, Mar. 13, 2003.

28. For the preceding four paragraphs, see Rice, "The Swedes," 265. For a discussion of Swedish classes in Minneapolis high schools, see Anita Olson Gustafson, "Teaching Swedish in the Public Schools: Cultural Persistence in Minneapolis," in *Swedes in the Twin Cities,* 223–39; information on Swedish at Minnehaha Academy is from the school administration.

29. For the preceding three paragraphs, see Rice, "The Swedes," 266. For accounts of Swan Turnblad and *Svenska Amerikanska Posten,* see Lewis, *American Swedish Institute,* 33–39, and Ulf Jonas Björk, "*Svenska Amerikanska Posten:* An Immigrant Newspaper with American Accents," in *Swedes in the Twin Cities,* 210–22. Early Swedish language newspapers are also discussed in Norelius, *Early Life of Eric Norelius,* Mattson, *Reminiscences,* and Emeroy Johnson, *Eric Norelius: Pioneer Midwest Pastor and Churchman* (Rock Island: Augustana Book Concern, 1954).

30. For the preceding six paragraphs, see Rice, "The Swedes," 266–67.

31. Information on Swedish classes was

obtained by the author via website catalogs, e-mail messages, and phone conversations with Gun Edberg-Caldwell, Swedish instructor at the University of Minnesota; Allison Spenader, dean of Sjölunden, Concordia Language Villages; Ewa Rydåker, one of the founders of *Svenska Skolan;* Gustavus Adolphus College; Bethel College; Barbro Roehrdanz, Swedish teacher at the American Swedish Institute.

32. For the preceding seven paragraphs, see Rice, "The Swedes," 267–68. For information on the evolution of the Evangelical Lutheran Church in America, see "Roots of the ELCA," www.elca.org. See Norelius, *Early Life of Eric Norelius,* for information on early Lutheran churches. See Lewis, *So Far Away in the World,* for information on Norelius, 117–20, Mount Olivet Lutheran Church in Minneapolis, 127, and Rev. William Hyllengren and Vasa Lutheran Church, 121–23.

33. For the Vasa Children's Home (later part of Lutheran Social Services), see Johnson, *Eric Norelius,* 132–35, 138–39; for the founding of Bethesda Hospital, see Lewis, *So Far Away in the World,* 117; for Augustana Church activities, see *125th Anniversary Celebration: Augustana Lutheran Church, 1866–1991* (Minneapolis: The Church, 1991). Materials on the Women's Missionary Society are in Region 3 Archives of the ELCA, Luther Seminary, St. Paul, especially see the society's 35th-anniversary publication.

34. Lewis, *So Far Away in the World,* 124–27.

35. The original minutes of the meetings of the Linnea Society, mainly in Swedish, are in the Linnea Home, St. Paul; copies (notebook P141), and a 1995 translation by John LaVine with information about the linen shower, MHS.

36. For gubernatorial campaigns, see Dag Blanck, "Swedish Americans and the 1918 Gubernatorial Campaign in Minnesota," 317–30, and Bruce L. Larson, "Gubernatorial Politics and Swedish Americans in Minnesota: The 1970 Election and Beyond," 331–49, both in *Swedes in the Twin Cities.*

37. A[lgot] E. Strand, ed., *A History of the Swedish-Americans of Minnesota* (Chicago: Lewis Pub. Co., 1910), 1:89–90, 93–94, 97.

38. For the preceding three paragraphs, see Rice, "The Swedes," 269–70.

39. A. Scott Berg, *Lindbergh* (New York: G.P. Putman's, 1998), 396; for a discussion of Lindbergh's speaking out for neutrality, see Berg, 384–432.

40. For the preceding five paragraphs, see Rice, "The Swedes," 270–71.

41. The American Swedish Institute Archives has information regarding *Svenska Bröderna* (the Swedish Brothers) that includes a 1907 directory giving the address of the building as 4th St. and 8th Ave. in Minneapolis and a copy of the Swedish song in which the "brothers" were admonished to help each other in time of need or be dismissed from membership: "Wherever you see a brother in need/to his aid you must quickly speed/and any one of us who ignores his plea/nevermore will a Swedish Brother be" (author's translation). For the Norden Society, see William C. Beyer, "Brothers Whether Dancing or Dying: Minneapolis's Norden Society, 1871–198?" in *Swedes in the Twin Cities,* 124–36.

42. For the preceding two paragraphs, see Rice, "The Swedes," 268–69.

43. For the preceding three paragraphs, see Rice, "The Swedes," 269; author's conversation with Bruce Karstadt, executive

director of the American Swedish Institute, April 29, 2003; information on events in various issues of *ASI Posten*.

44. Author's conversation with Elise Peters, a member of *Nyckleharpalag,* May 14, 2003.

45. Hans Mattson, *250th Anniversary of the First Swedish Settlement in America. September 14, 1888* (Minneapolis, 1889), 3.

46. Rice, "The Swedes," 271; for the Swedish Council of America, see www.swedishcouncil.org; Lewis, *So far Away in the World,* 103.

47. Author's conversation with Lynne Moratzka, www.scandiamn.com, and brochures regarding the site.

48. Rice, "The Swedes," 271; www.brainerd.net/~pwilson/nisswastamman.

49. Rice, "The Swedes," 272.

50. Rice, "The Swedes," 272; *Minneapolis Star Tribune,* July 27, 2003, p. 8B.

Notes to Sidebars

Swedish Meatballs, p. 2: Recipes from Arlene Gronvall and Lorraine McGrath.

Vasa, p. 8: Johnson, *Eric Norelius,* 272, 101, 68, 70; Mattson, *Reminiscences,* 99, 61,116, 143; Lewis, *American Swedish Institute,* 13, 33–39, 9, back cover; Alexander P. Anderson, Notebooks, 1899–1931 (M314), MHS.

Exploring Their Swedish Heritage, p. 10: Author's conversations with the Olander sisters, Corrine Hasse of Chaska and Vernis Strom of Chanhassen, winter 2003. The sisters shared both their memories and copies of their great-grandfather's Civil War service records.

Cooperative Creameries, p. 15: Author's conversation with Jane Videen of Shafer; Jack El-Hai, *Celebrating Tradition, Building the Future: Seventy-five Years of Land O' Lakes* (Minneapolis: Land O' Lakes,

Inc.,1996), 13, 16, 18; Marlys Wickstrom and R. W. Dutch Schoenecker, *Preserving a Sense of Heritage: Isanti, Minnesota Centennial, 1899–1999* (Coon Rapids: ECM Publishers, Inc., 1998), 36, 108.

A Ship Full of Swedes, p. 24: Duluth Weekly Minnesotian, June 19, 1869, May 25, 1872; author's conversation with Pat Maus, Northeast Minnesota Historical Center, Duluth.

The Carlson Sisters, p. 27: Author's conversations with Dana Heimark, Ramsey House, who portrays Sophie Carlson in living history presentations; Governor Ramsey's journals and letters, specifically his journal, Sept. 24, 1876; Marion Furness to Charles Furness, R27F283 (Aug. 4, 1882); journal entries, R44 F357 (May 5, 1886), R44 F145 (Sept. 9, 1885), R44 F145 (Nov. 14, 1885), R44 F719 (Jan. 20, 1888), R44 F1001 (June 19, 1889)—all Alexander Ramsey and Family Personal Papers and Governor's Records, 1829–1965, MHS. The letter from Carl Englund is in *En Smålandssocken Emigrerar: En bok om emigrationen till Amerika* (Växjö: Långasjö, 1967), 825.

The Cuban Connection, p. 28: Marilyn McGriff, "Minnesota Swedes Raising Cane," *Minnesota History* 56 (Spring 1999): 288, 292, 294, 296–98; 1913 postcard from S. P. Anderson, in possession of Karen Lood; author's conversations and correspondence with Karen Lood, fall 2002, winter and spring 2003.

The Akerlund Photo Studio, p. 36: Author's conversations with Mike Worcester, Akerlund Photo Studio, Cokato; Mike Worcester, "Gust Akerlund: Cokato Photographer," *Swedish American Genealogist* 19 (March 1997): 15–20.

Marlys and Family, p. 38: Author's conversation with Marlys Wickstrom, Cambridge, spring 2003. Marlys later sent her this poem.

Salvation Army, p. 40: Edward O. Nelson, *Hallelujah!! Recollection of Salvation Army Scandinavian Work in the U.S.A.* (Chicago: The Salvation Army, 1987), 74 (quote), 18, 1, 29, 143–47, copy in American Swedish Institute; William A. Johnson, *O Boundless Salvation, the Story of the Scandinavian Salvation Army in the United States,* (New York, 1988), 4 (quote), 16 (quote); *Genom 45 År, Återblick över Frälsningsarmens skandinaviska arvete i Amerika, 1887–1933* (Chicago, 1933), 75 (quote); Nelson, 133. Author's conversations with Mavis Teska, granddaughter of drummer Otto Pearson.

The Moberg Mystique, p. 69: Author's conversations with Alice and John Mortenson, fall 2002. Ewa Rydåker, who leads tours of Swedish-American sites in Chisago County, has told the author of a few individuals on the tours who believe that Moberg's characters are historic rather than fictional. For information on *Kristina från Duvemåla,* see www.duvemala. com; Jan McElfish, American Swedish Institute, provided performance information regarding *Kristina från Duvemåla.*

Index

Page numbers in italic refer to pictures and captions.

Picture Credits

Names of the photographers, when known, are in parentheses.

Page 6, 8 (both; bottom, Lawson Studios, Chicago), 15 (Palm-quist Studio), 19, 21, 22 (bottom), 25, 27 (collection of the Ramsey House), 30, 31, 32(David Peterson, Princeton), 36 (Mike Melman), 47 (Seth Cedarholm, Marine), 53(Charles J. Hibbard, Metropolitan Medical Center), 55, 57 (both; left, Anton M. Opsahl; right, Benjamin C. Golling), 58 (Lee Brothers), 62 (Norton and Peel), 63 (Minneapolis Star-Journal-Tribune), 67—Minnesota Historical Society

Page x, 38—Marlys Wickstrom

Page 2—Linda Gronvall

Page 5—Ken Johnson

Page 9, 52—Goodhue County Historical Society

Page 10—Corrine Hasse and Vernis Strom

Page 13—Isanti County Historical Society

Page 16—Audrey Johnson

Page 18—Arne Everson

Page 22 (top)—Gloria Anderson-Hegg

Page 23, 39—Lawrence Hammerstrom

Page 28—Karen Lood

Page 35, 43—Minneapolis Public Library, Minneapolis Collection

Page 40—Mavis Teska

Page 42 (both)—Gustavus Adolphus College, St. Peter

Page 44, 64 (Jan McElfish)—American Swedish Institute, Minneapolis

Page 49 (V. S. Arrowsmith)—Time Travel

Page 50 (Gust Akerlund)—Akerlund Collection, Cokato Museum

Page 60—Kittson County Historical Society

Page 66—Flickorna Fem

Page 68—Jane Videen

Page 69 (Alice Mortenson)—Nya Duvemåla

Page 70 (Jonathan Chapman)—Vasaloppet, Mora

Page 74—Private Collection

Acknowledgments

I am indebted to John G. Rice, who did the excellent research for and wrote the original chapter, "The Swedes," in *They Chose Minnesota* on which this revised and expanded work is based. I owe a big *tack så mycket* to the staff at the American Swedish Institute in Minneapolis, including Bruce Karstadt, Marita Karlisch, Jan McElfish, and Nina Clark for their encouragement and help with research. Thanks also to staff members at many historical museums in Minnesota, especially those in Goodhue, Isanti, Kanabec, Kandiyohi, Kittson, and Marshall Counties, Mike Worcester at the Cokato Museum and Akerlund Photo Studio, *Nya Duvemåla* in Lindstrom, *Gammelgården* in Scandia, the James J. Hill Archives, Paul Daniels at the ELCA Region 3 Archives, and Pat Maus and her volunteers at the Northeast Minnesota Historical Center in Duluth, for answering questions and making excellent suggestions for further research. My own circle of Swedes—Ewa Rydåker, Inger Pignolet, Lois Anderson, Mariann Tiblin, Ken Johnson, Larry Hammerstrom, Marlys Wickstrom, Audrey Johnson, Karen Lood, Jean Ross, Valorie Arrowsmith, John and Alice Mortenson, and Lorraine McGrath, among others—provided both good cheer and good stories, many of which are in this book. Many others have told me tales of their Swedish immigrant ancestors and shown me photographs and other memorabilia that have provided a kind of background tapestry for my research. A special thanks to Linda Gronvall for providing the family story and recipe that opens this book, to the Olander sisters, Corrine Olander Hasse and Vernis Olander Strom, for their reminiscences, Bud Erickson for the story about his grandmother, Jane Videen for creamery information, Glorias Anderson and Swanson for their help, and Alice Sjoquist for coffee, conversation, and raspberries! From start to finish, my editor, Sally Rubinstein, and her colleagues at the Minnesota Historical Society, Debbie Miller and Dana Heimark, have made writing this book an enjoyable experience. And, as always, I would like to thank my husband, Stephen Lewis, for his support and encouragement.

Minnesotans can trace their families and their state's heritage to a multitude of ethnic groups. *The People of Minnesota* series tells each group's story in a compact, handsomely illustrated, and accessible paperback. Readers will learn about the group's accomplishments, ethnic organizations, settlement patterns, and occupations. Each book includes a personal story of one person or family, told through a diary, a letter, or an oral history.

In his introduction to the series, Bill Holm reminds us why these stories are as important as ever: "To be ethnic, somehow, is to be human. Neither can we escape it, nor should we want to. You cannot interest yourself in the lives of your neighbors if you don't take sufficient interest in your own."

This series is based on the critically acclaimed book *They Chose Minnesota: A Survey of the State's Ethnic Groups* (Minnesota Historical Society Press). The volumes in *The People of Minnesota* bring each group's story up to date and add dozens of photographs to inform and enhance the telling.

Books in the series include *Irish in Minnesota, Jews in Minnesota, Norwegians in Minnesota, African Americans in Minnesota, Germans in Minnesota,* and *Chinese in Minnesota.*

Bill Holm is the grandson of four Icelandic immigrants to Minneota, Minnesota, where he still lives. He is the author of eight books including *Eccentric Island: Travels Real and Imaginary* and *Coming Home Crazy.* When he is not practicing the piano or on the road circuit-riding for literature, he teaches at Southwest State University in Marshall, Minnesota.

About the Author

Anne Gillespie Lewis is a Minneapolis journalist and author of several books, including *So Far Away in the World: Stories from the Swedish Twin Cities* and *The American Swedish Institute: Turnblad's Castle.*